THE HIGH SCHOOLER'S GUIDE TO MONEY

THAN MERRILL
and
JP SERVIDEO

The High Schooler's Guide to Money
J.P. Servideo & Than Merrill
Published by FortuneBuilders, Inc

FortuneBuilders, Inc
960 Grand Ave
San Diego, CA 92109
E-mail: guidetomoneybook@gmail.com

Limit of Liability / Disclaimer of Warranty:

While the publisher and author have used their best efforts in preparing this book, they make no representations or warranties with respect to the accuracy or completeness of the contents of this book and specifically disclaim any implied warranties of merchantability or fitness for a particular purpose. No warranty may be created or extended by sales representatives or written sales materials. The advice and strategies contained herein may not be suitable for your situation. You should consult with a professional when appropriate. Neither the publisher nor the author shall be liable for any loss of profit or any other commercial damages, including but not limited to special, incidental, consequential, or other damages.

Publishing and editorial team: Author Bridge Media,
www.AuthorBridgeMedia.com
Project Manager and Editorial Director: Helen Chang
Editor: Katherine MacKenett
Publishing Manager: Laurie Aranda
Publishing Assistant: Iris Sasing

Library of Congress Control Number: 2017945530
ISBN: 978-0-9991166-0-9 -- paperback
978-0-9991166-1-6 -- hardcover
978-0-9991166-2-3 -- ebook

Ordering Information:

Quantity sales. Special discounts are available on quantity purchases by corporations, associations, and others. For details, contact the publisher at the address above.

Printed in the United States of America

DEDICATIONS

THAN'S DEDICATION:

This book is dedicated to you. If you have picked it up to increase your financial intelligence, I applaud you and look forward to helping you achieve that goal.

JP'S DEDICATION:

This is for the kids who say "Give me the ball" with the game on the line—and the ones who want to. Anyone can change the world. You will be the ones who do it.

CONTENTS

ACKNOWLEDGMENTS

THAN'S ACKNOWLEDGMENTS:

I would like to express my deepest gratitude to the many coaches and mentors I have had the pleasure of learning from over the years who taught me many of the principles I share within this book.

I would also like to thank our dedicated team members who work at FortuneBuilders Inc.; CT Homes, LLC; and Grand Coast Capital. Your efforts and dedication to our coaching students and real estate investor clients are remarkable. Each of you has contributed ideas that JP Servideo and I share in this book, and we appreciate the contribution you make to our clients' success each and every day.

I would also like to thank my longtime friends and teammates Paul Esajian, Konrad Sopielnikow, Geoff Chadwick, Noah Cosby, JD Esajian, and Ralph Plumb. I appreciate your friendship and loyalty.

I would like to thank JP Servideo, my coauthor, for pushing this book to the finish line and for his consistent dedication to the mission.

Finally, I would like to thank my wife, my partner, the mother of my children, and my best friend, Cindy Phillips. You are my rock.

JP'S ACKNOWLEDGMENTS:

This book never would have happened if I hadn't become the person I am today. I am that person because of where I'm from, where I've been, and most importantly because of the people I've met along this unpredictable journey. I want to take a second to thank those people.

First, thank you to my family. You can't choose your family, and with one as big as mine, you go through a lot over the years, but I love you all. I have missed holidays and events and haven't had too much time to visit between speaking engagements. I want you all to know that I care about you deeply, and I am working toward building something that will resonate through generations to come. Thank you for your endless love.

Mom, the way you battled through adversity our entire young lives inspired me and gave me strength. Your unconditional love and support is where I get my drive and determination to succeed. Thank you. Words do my gratitude no justice.

I'm grateful to my friends in Boston and around the globe—the ones who never wavered in their loyalty and belief in me, the ones who were family when mine was three thousand miles away, and the ones whose families became part of my own. I've built my character on the (good and bad) decisions we made and how we handled the results, together.

To Than, Paul, J.D., Konrad, the entire FortuneBuilders family, and everyone who played a part in getting me here, thank you. I was always a big dreamer. I always knew I would be successful, and although I still have a long way to go, this family showed me the path to everything I always knew was possible. You all inspire me daily.

Thank you to Jon Steingraber for adamantly asking me to partner on the first Future FortuneBuilders camp with him. Thank you to Rachel for making sure we followed through with it, even when Jon couldn't participate anymore. Thank you to Mannie for meeting with me over the last three-plus years, sometimes weekly, to discuss how we could keep this movement going. And to the volunteers, room managers, people who helped build presentations, and those who have helped to promote our cause, there are too many of you to name, but I thank you all!

Thank you also to Josh, Clint, and my fellow mastermind members, who have helped me develop my voice and communicate my message.

Finally, I want to thank Katherine MacKenett, Helen Chang, and the team at Author Bridge Media. The way you took hours of stories, presentations, facts, and statistics and put them into this easily digestible book—all while making the process so easy, fun, and efficient—was a feat. Thank you for helping with everything I didn't know how to do to get this book to the finish line.

INTRODUCTION

The Trap

Look, we get it. You probably don't want to be reading this right now.

We admit we could be wrong. Maybe you can't wait to learn all about how money works. Someone put this book in your hands, and you were like, "Heck yes, bring it *on*."

But if you're like most of the high schoolers we meet, you're probably not that excited about it. Maybe you're kind of interested in money, but let's face it: you can get money from your mom or dad, and you have better things to do than learn about how it works. You'd rather be playing video games or catching the latest Marvel movie with your friends. But reading a book about something you probably don't even have much of yet? Most likely not your idea of a fun Friday night.

Which means that if you're reading this at all, someone's probably making you do it. And the fact that they're *making you do it* is exactly the problem. Because come on, admit it.

You're sick of everyone telling you what to do.

You've got parents telling you to clean your room or to take out the trash or to "put the phone down and go get some fresh air, for crying out loud." You've got teachers controlling your life eight hours a day—and then sending you home with more work to do at night and on the weekends. Frankly, you've had it with doing what *they* want you to do all the time.

You want to do what *you* want to do.

You get that these people mean well, but that's not the point. *You're* the one who knows what makes *you* happy. Maybe you're even counting down the days until you escape all the parents and teachers, and you're finally *free*. You won't live at home anymore, and no one will know or care if you clean your stupid room. You can go wherever you want to go, do whatever you want to do. Finally, your life will truly be *yours*.

Well, sort of.

Because here's what they don't tell you about the whole graduating-and-moving-out-of-the-house thing. Yeah, it's true that you're free of parents and teachers when you make your great escape. But when they hand off the reins of your freedom, they don't pass them to you.

They put them in the hands of a new overlord: money.

Meet Your New Overlord: Money

Here's what really happens:

You move out, and you're free to make your own decisions. But you're still not free to do whatever you want. Why?

Because you don't have the money to do whatever you want. Instead, you have rent. You have bills. You've got to go out and get the money to pay for those things.

And that's when you kind of become a slave to your job.

Your job controls you because it controls how much money you make. It tells you what you can and can't do, what you can and can't buy. Even if you're a young entrepreneur, your business is still the one controlling you—not the other way around.

No matter how you earn it, you're always controlled by the income that you do or do not have. Eventually you start to think, "Hey, I want to do and buy more things." And what does that take? More money. Then, the more things you have, the harder you have to work to support that lifestyle.

It becomes a vicious cycle. And the worst part is that most people never get off this hamster wheel.

Most people don't learn how money works until it's too late. By the time they realize it's an issue, they're in their twenties, thirties, or forties, and either they have to struggle to make up for lost time, or they can't catch up at all.

You think you've got time to figure this out, but the scary thing is, you don't. Not really. If you don't learn about money now, you're probably going to stay stuck under other people's control for a very long time. That's what happens to most people. Most people never experience true freedom in their entire lives.

Here's some good news, though: you don't have to be most people.

The Way Out

There is a way out of the money trap. And it's actually incredibly simple.

All you have to do is understand how money works.

Understanding how money works is not crazy hard. It's not even that complicated. You don't have to be a genius to understand money. It's like playing Monopoly. Anyone who knows the rules can play. As soon as you know the rules, it's anyone's game.

Once you understand money, you become the master of *it*, instead of letting it be the master of *you*. And when that happens, guess what? Money no longer equals lifelong slavery.

Money equals freedom.

Instead of you having to work hard for money all the

time, money starts working for you instead—just because of where you put it. As a friend of ours likes to say, "I want my money to leave and bring me back more friends in the form of interest." That's exactly what money can do for you when you know how it works. You can send it on a mission to find more money and bring it back to you without you having to actually do anything.

Meanwhile, if your money is doing all this work for you . . . what are you doing?

Answer: *anything you want.* You don't have to worry about covering your expenses. You're not locked into a job. If you go to work and realize you don't love what you're doing, you don't have to stay. When you have more money coming in than you have expenses going out, you're free to pursue anything you want.

In other words, you can do what you want, all the time. You can live your passion, volunteer, travel. You can find your highest calling. If you want to take a few vacations a year, you can. If you want to move from New York to California, go for it. If you want to drop everything and backpack through Europe—yeah, you can do that, too.

You can experience life. Why?

Because once you become the master of your money, *no one can tell you what to do.* Not your parents, not your teachers, not your job—no one.

Finally, you have true freedom. And the earlier you learn how money works, the faster everything you want can be yours. Bottom line: life is way more fun if you learn all this stuff about money now, instead of when you're in your twenties or thirties. Trust us. We know.

Who Are We and How Do We Know What We're Talking About?

We are Than Merrill and JP Servideo, real estate investors, friends, and coaches at FortuneBuilders, a financial education company that teaches people how to invest in real estate and other kinds of assets. And we know all this about money because we had to learn it ourselves—the hard way.

Than's Story

I never really thought about money until I almost lost it all.

When I was twenty-three years old, my lifelong dream came true: I had the opportunity to play in the NFL for two seasons. And I loved it. Unfortunately, though, the only thing harder than making it to the NFL is staying in the NFL.

After I was injured and then subsequently cut, my dream came to an abrupt end. And so did my NFL paycheck.

I had taken pretty much everything I had saved

after my first year in the NFL—which was just under $100,000—and invested most of it into a Mexican grill. After getting cut, I fell back on managing the restaurant. It was the only thing I had.

What I didn't realize was that the restaurant business will chew you up and spit you out if you're not educated in the industry. By the next year, I realized that if I didn't do something quickly, the restaurant was going to consume the little money that I had left.

For the first time in my life, money became a priority.

I began to study how to make money and how to invest it. As I did, I fell in love with the process—especially with how to invest in real estate. Before long, I realized that I had a lot more passion for real estate than I did for making burritos. So I sold the restaurant at a loss and never looked back.

More than fourteen years later, I've invested in and bought and sold hundreds of millions of dollars of real estate. My investments make a sizable amount of passive income through my real estate company, CT Homes, LLC. I've founded several other real estate companies, including FortuneBuilders, which has helped thousands of people get started investing in real estate.

The things I know about money now are the things I wish I had known when I was in high school. I teamed up with JP to write this book and build our Future FortuneBuilders program because I believe that education leads to a better future. And I want you to be able to achieve success just like we have, using the same tool we used to get there: money.

JP's Story

One of my earliest memories is about money.

I was eight years old. My parents had just gotten divorced, and my mom, my two sisters, and I had moved to this really not nice area of town in Massachusetts. We weren't *in* the projects, but they were right across the street.

While we were living there, I remember my mom saying to us one night, "Hey guys, we're going to play a game! All of us are going to run around the house and see who can gather up the most change. Then we can go to McDonald's for dinner!"

My mom's old school; she cooks everything. We never ate fast food. As I walked around the house, looking for nickels under loose papers and couch cushions, I thought, "I'm pretty sure that if we don't find this change, we can't eat, because I don't think we have any other money today."

That was the moment I knew I had to find a way out. I was only in second grade, but that didn't matter. Someday, I knew I'd find a way to make enough money so my family would never have to feel like we did that evening ever again. It took a lot of years of trying and failing to figure it out, but in my mind I always knew that I would be successful. And today I am.

I've made more than six figures in income for the past several years, and now I know how to make that money work for me. I'm so into this success and money stuff that I travel around the country sharing what I've learned with other people. Yahoo! Finance, CBS 7 in San Diego, *TheStreet*, and a bunch of other publications have all featured the work I do. They call it "a national initiative for financial literacy." I've helped the homeless, given away scholarships to the Boys & Girls Clubs, and traveled to almost twenty countries and to every state in the United States.

I have talked to thousands of high school kids and their parents about money. But honestly? I'm not writing this book for you.

I'm writing it for fifteen-year-old me.

I'm one of those people who didn't learn how money worked until later in the game. Sure, I'm doing the things I need to do now, but even I can't take the same approach that you're able to take. I have to work a lot harder to get where I want to go, and it's going to take me more time. But if I could start over, I'd tell fifteen-year-old me everything that Than and I are going to share with you in this book. I'd take the easy road to freedom instead of the uphill climb.

Listen, I'm not saying you have to do this one way or the other. I'm just saying that right now, you still have a choice. You can still take the easy route. In just a few years, that path will be gone for you like it disappeared for me.

Which road would you rather take?

Your Road Map to Freedom

This book isn't going to tell you what to do with your money. It's going to tell you how money works so that you know how to buy your own freedom fastest—however that works for you.

Here's how to get the most out of the hundred pages you're about to read:

First, go through the whole thing start to finish. Just read it. (It won't take that long—promise. It took us only two hours to read it for the first time after we finished writing it.) If you see stuff that really strikes a chord with you, highlight it. Then, after you finish the book, go back to the things that sounded important to you or the things you didn't understand as much and give them some more thought.

The more lightbulbs go on as you're reading this, the more you'll understand money. The more you understand money, the faster your life will finally belong to you.

You're not going to do all this stuff at once. It happens one step at a time. Let these chapters be a guide that you keep going back to every time you're ready to take one more step forward. When it's time to create a budget, go back to the budget chapter and put those resources into action. Same with setting goals. Same with investing and retirement accounts and everything else. The important thing is to *do* something with this knowledge once you have it.

We designed this book to be your road map to the life you want for yourself, whatever it may look like. Whether you get on the road and start driving is up to you.

The Money Tree

Money might not grow on trees, but it does grow *like* one. Plant a seed now, and it will turn into something huge twenty years from now.

No seed is too small to plant, either. You don't need a lot of money to get started. The tricks you'll learn in this book are things you'll be able to do the second any money comes your way, whether it comes from a birthday card, a holiday gift, or a summer job. Every bit of money counts—and so does every bit of time. Every single day that goes by (yes, even while you're still in high school) equals a significant amount of money later.

It doesn't matter if you've never had money before. You don't have to be a genius to understand this stuff. No matter where you come from, the color of your skin, or the environment you grew up in, if you understand how money works, you can have the life you want. Because again, money is like Monopoly: as soon as you know what the rules are, it's anyone's game. This book is going to show you what the rules are in the game of money. After that, you can play the game however you want.

What are you going to win if you decide to play?

You're going to win true freedom. You're going to win real independence, lifelong security, and happiness. You're going to win everything you ever wanted—and then some. You're going to win your own life, plain and simple.

Understand how money works, and then do something about it. Right now.

Chapter 1

WHAT IS MONEY?

Our acts can be no wiser than our thoughts. Our thinking can be no wiser than our understanding.
—*George S. Clason in*
The Richest Man in Babylon

What Is Money?

What is money, really?

It's not just dollars and coins and credit cards. It's not a bunch of numbers on a bank statement. Those things are just what money *looks* like.

What money really *is*, though, is a vehicle for freedom.

You can say money doesn't buy happiness, and you're absolutely right. But it does buy time. When you have money, you can own your own time. Owning your time is true freedom. And hey, let's face it: when you have true freedom, it's a lot easier to be happy.

Do you need money to be happy? No. But money is an absolute necessity to have freedom—100 percent.

Most people live their lives as slaves to money. They have to work for it. But the wealthiest people don't. The wealthiest people leverage money to own their time and gain freedom. They do that by using math, because that's another thing that money is: a bunch of formulas. If you understand the formulas and follow them, you'll get to where you want to be.

You know what money isn't, though? Bad.

Anyone who tells you that money is the root of all evil probably doesn't have it. People with money are not bad people. They just did different things with their money—things that anyone else could have done.

Things that you can do.

In this chapter, we'll show you why everything you've been taught about money might not be true. We'll also let you in on the habits of the wealthiest people in the world—things everyday people can do—and show you how caring about money now can literally set you free for the rest of your life.

Why Everything They Told You about Money Is (Probably) Wrong

If anyone has ever tried to teach you about money, the odds are pretty good that the lesson sounded something like this: go to college, get a good job, save your money, and you'll be set.

And the thing is, the person who taught you that probably wasn't wrong. That story used to be true. For your grandparents' and maybe even for your parents' generation, that path worked. A good education got you a good job, and you worked at that job—for one company—for forty years until you retired with a gold watch and a pension. That path used to be a real thing. Which is probably why your parents or grandparents gave you this advice in the first place: because they followed it themselves, and they did okay in the end.

Nowadays, however, that advice doesn't work. Laws have changed. Companies have changed. Pensions are no longer available. And hey, no one wears gold watches anymore. Back in the day, you could be a middle-class family who paid off your house, paid off your expenses, had a pension, and lived comfortably. But in the last few decades, that way of life has disappeared—and the middle class has disappeared with it.

What does this mean for you?

It means that in the future, people are going to be either wealthy or poor—and you get to choose which one of those you want to be. Which prompts the next question: What makes people wealthy, rich, or poor?

How Wealth Works (the Power of Passive Income)

Okay, so if the save-up-and-retire model doesn't cut it anymore, what does? What actually makes you wealthy these days?

Answer: It's what you choose to *do* with your money. Specifically, it has to do with a little thing called passive income.

Passive income is also called "mailbox money." It's money you don't have to trade your time for. You could be traveling the world and not working at a job, and this money would still come to you. Most passive income comes from things you invest in, which are called assets. A great example would be purchasing a rental property. The property would be your asset, and the money your renters paid you every month would be your passive income—your "mailbox money."

The reason most people are poor instead of wealthy is simple: they don't put enough money into assets that will give them passive income. Instead, they spend it on other things. Take a look at this chart:

Default Look

The middle column in the chart is your job, or active income—money you have to work for. On the left you have your assets, or passive income. And on the right you have your liabilities, which are things that cost you money.

What happens first—for everybody, wealthy or poor— is that the middle column grows. You go out and you make some money. After that, the road splits.

Poor Look

Poor people take the money they made, and they put it in their liabilities column. They get a car, an apartment, a hundred-dollar pair of jeans. Then the middle column grows again, and the liabilities column keeps growing with it: they buy a nicer car, a house, a new wardrobe—maybe take a vacation to Tahiti. They're not free, because they have to work for all that stuff. But they're getting by.

Then something happens—the economy crashes, they lose their job, or they have a sudden and costly illness. Suddenly, we put a big red X through that middle column. No more money is coming in. What's left?

A lot of liabilities that still need to be paid for. And no way to pay for them.

That's when they discover that they've literally become

a slave to the things that they have to pay off. Their whole lives, they built up that right column as fast as they could, and then they got stuck maintaining it. When the middle column disappears, it's scary. "Holy cow, what do I do now?" they think.

Now, here's how the wealthiest people do it.

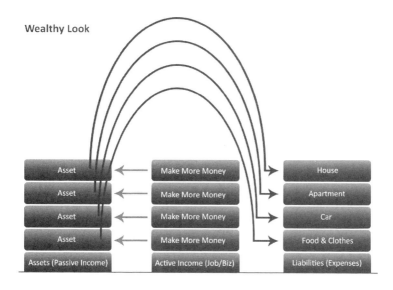

They start out with the same three columns as everybody else. But the difference is that when their middle column grows, they put their money into the left column—the assets column. That earns them some passive income. And the one to the right? Their liabilities column? It goes only as high as the assets column grows.

What does that mean?

It means that if we put another big red X through the middle column, their liabilities are still paid for—by passive income. If their active-income job disappears, it's not a big deal. They're not tied to their job; they don't *have* to do anything. All because their liabilities never rise beyond their asset threshold.

It's like when you are playing a video game and you hit a checkpoint. If you die after you hit it, it's not a big deal. You just go back to that checkpoint. Same thing for people who never let their liabilities go higher than their assets. They basically get the safety of checkpoints their entire lives.

Are these people rich? Not necessarily. Rich means having a lot of money. Wealthy means having a lot of time. Wealthy people own their time, which means they have true freedom. And they own it just by having a mindset of putting money toward assets first—before they buy the fancy cars and nice houses and expensive vacations.

This is how you can retire by thirty—or by any age you want, really. Most people think retirement is a big lump sum of money. It's not. Retirement is just owning your time, and to own your time, all you need is more income coming in than you have going out. That's it.

You don't have to have a ton of money to be wealthy. The second your passive income is greater than your expenses, you have wealth. And if you train your brain to think about money this way now, you will be wealthy for the rest of your life.

Why Money Matters *Now*

Most high schoolers we talk to aren't that excited about money. Yeah, you'd like to have some extra money to spend, but you don't have any expenses. You have everything you need to live.

So you feel like you have time. You feel like you don't need to do this money thing right now. You may not have even had a job yet. Why should you care about what to do with income you don't even have? You can worry about it when you get to college or when you start working. Right?

Sure you can. This is your life. You can do whatever you want with it. We're not here to tell you what to do.

But the wealthiest people don't worry about money later. They start thinking about it as early as they can, for two reasons: math and science.

The Math: Compound Interest

Like we said, you don't have to do any of this money stuff right now. But here's what happens if you do: compound interest.

The fancy definition of compound interest is "the rule of seventy-two." It's the formula for how long money takes to grow on its own. Seventy-two divided by the interest rate you're getting equals how much time it will take your money to double.

So that's the fancy definition. The simple definition is this: compound interest is about putting your money in a place where it can grow—even if you're just setting a little bit of it aside every time you make some. Compound interest takes the very small financial decisions you make from a very young age and turns them into enormous freedom and luxuries later in life.

It gives you more wealth than you could ever imagine. That's why compound interest is the single most important thing you can learn about money as a high schooler.

How big of a difference does it make, really?

Well, money guru Dave Ramsey tells this story about it. You have two friends, Ben and Arthur, and they decide that they're each going to invest $2,000 a year. The difference is *when* they start making those investments. Ben starts when he's nineteen and invests $2,000 every year until he turns twenty-six. Then he stops. So Ben invests $16,000 total, over eight years.

Meanwhile, Arthur doesn't start investing his $2,000 a year until he turns twenty-seven. Then he keeps putting in that same $2,000 yearly until he turns sixty-four. So Arthur spends thirty-nine years and $78,000 on his investments.

When Ben and Arthur turn sixty-five, they compare

their investments. Arthur's money grew from $78,000 into $1.5 million. Not bad, right? But guess what happened to Ben's money?

Ben's investment of $16,000 turned into $2.2 million. And he never invested a dime after he turned twenty-six. That means Ben ended up with $700,000 more, and he had to do only a fraction of the work to get it. (We'll tell you everything you need to know about investing in chapter 4, by the way.)

Here's a diagram that shows how compound interest works:

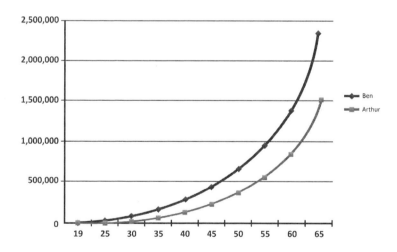

If you want to figure out how to make compound interest work for you personally, you can also check out our compound interest calculator at www.futurefortunebuilders. com.

So do you have to start thinking about money now? No. But is it a whole lot easier to become wealthy if you *do* get started early?

Yes. Yes it is.

The Science: How to Outsmart Your Brain

Compound interest is great, but it's not the only reason to start thinking about finances now. Because money isn't just math; it's also science.

According to the June 2015 issue of *Scientific American*, the reason most people don't start thinking about money until they're in their twenties has to do with brain development. Your brain has two parts: the limbic side, which controls emotion, and the prefrontal cortex, which controls logic. Up until you hit puberty, these two parts are balanced. Then, when you hit your early teens, your emotional brain takes a huge leap forward. Your logical brain catches up eventually, but not until you're in your mid-twenties.

In the meantime, two things happen.

First, you automatically react to things more from emotion than from logic. And second, while the connection between these two parts of your brain is elastic—like wet cement—you form habits. Habits that you'll take with you into your adult life.

(What happens with a lot of people is that they just

let the emotional brain launch its hostile takeover without a fight. Sure, thinking about money might make sense—but they just don't *feel* like it. So they let it go. Putting it off becomes a habit that sticks to them once they become adults. Then, if they ever break free of the habit at all, it's usually much too late to catch up.)

Which means that, right now, you have an awesome opportunity. You have the opportunity to *outsmart your emotional brain* by not always doing what it tells you to do. Instead, you can form good money habits that will make you wealthy *for the rest of your life*.

The catch is that you're probably not going to feel like doing any of this stuff. You have to fight the emotion. That's the hard part. But in the end, it pays off—literally.

When you control your brain, you control your results. And when the result is money, what you're really controlling is your own freedom. Plain and simple.

The Road to True Wealth

If you understand money, you can make sound financial decisions. The better financial decisions you make, the more freedom you'll have. And the more freedom you have, the better your life will be.

In the rest of this book, we'll be showing you the road to true wealth, paved by the wealthy before us. We're not going to tell you how to drive it; that's up to you. We just want you to understand the road signs so that you can get where you want to go as fast as possible. Just because you're not reinventing the wheel doesn't mean you can't put your own rims on it.

Here are the seven "road signs" we'll be looking at.

Financial Literacy 101. If you want to play baseball, you need some basic equipment first: a bat, a mitt, a helmet. The same is true with money. Before you can make it work for you, you need some basic tools. We'll introduce you to the fundamental terms people use when they talk about money so that you have the knowledge you need to understand how everything works together.

Your Budget and the Four Buckets. You can't figure out how to get where you want to go until you know where you are. Your budget and the four buckets will show you what your current location is on the road to wealth—and tell you what the first step is on the way to your destination.

Investing. Investing is the key to passive income. But investing itself can seem complicated when you first look into it. We'll show you what your most common options are and explain exactly what each investment is, what its average rates of return are, and what the general fees are to invest in each option. From there, you can choose where to invest, so you can start making money with your money.

Credit. Credit is a way to leverage other people's money. We'll show you how you can do that safely, so you can build a great credit score, save tons of money on interest, and grow your passive income—and own your freedom—faster.

Taxes. As the saying goes, "The only things guaranteed in life are death and taxes." With taxes, it's not about how much you make; it's about how much you keep. Your taxes are the biggest bill you'll ever have, but most people know nothing about them. We'll give you the basics you need to understand about taxes, so you can keep more money in your pocket.

Student Loans. A lot of high schoolers go to college and take out loans without thinking about it. Then they get burned when they graduate and have to pay them back with huge amounts of interest. But if you understand how student loans work, you can plan for that expense and save as much money as possible for your education. We'll break down the different kinds of student loans for you and show you how much they cost.

Giving Back. The most successful people understand that one of the greatest uses of wealth is
making other lives better. Warren Buffett, Bill
Gates—these guys have literally pledged more than
90 percent of their wealth to solving the world's
problems. When you help others become better
versions of themselves, you experience the real
endgame of wealth and freedom: true fulfillment.

The principles of money will never change. Have certain strategies evolved? Yes. But the most important concepts are the same today as they were a hundred years ago.
If you understand the basic facts, you'll be fine, regardless
of where you come from, who you are, or what you do.

The road to true wealth isn't hard to travel. You just
have to know that it's there, and then you need to choose
to walk it—starting with the first step on the journey to
true freedom: financial literacy 101.

Chapter 2

FINANCIAL LITERACY 101

If we're not talking large money, what's the point?

—Jay-Z

Start Your Engines

Fun fact: more than 210 million people drive cars in the United States. That's about two-thirds of the total population.

But how many of those people actually know how to build an engine?

Probably not that many. Most people don't even know what all the different parts of an engine are called, let alone understand how to build one. If our national culture said, "You have to build your own engine in order to drive a car," how many people would actually drive one? Very few.

It sounds crazy, but this is the situation with money today.

Right now, everyone in the world has some money, but hardly anyone knows exactly how it works. We don't even know what the parts of the money engine are called. Could we learn that this is a spark plug and that's a piston if we wanted to? Sure, but none of us wants to bother. So we just start putting our engines together without knowing what we're doing, and when we're finished, our cars don't drive. That's why it's a good idea to know what all the moving parts of money are.

That's why we need financial literacy.

Financial Literacy 101

"Financial literacy" sounds complicated, but it's just a basic understanding of how money works. What are the moving parts of money, and how do they fit together?

Financial literacy matters because, just like you can't drive a car without a working engine, you can't have true wealth without understanding money. You can chug along with a badly built engine, and you might get by. But you won't get far.

If you take the time to figure out what all the different parts of the engine are and what they do, though, that's a different story. Now you know how the machine works. You can build a kickass engine from scratch, and you can fix it if it ever breaks or stalls on you. You never have to worry about having to take a badly made engine apart and rebuild it—or being too old to drive once you finally get it running right.

Instead, you can focus on the road—and on getting to your destination of wealth and freedom as fast as possible, with fewer detours.

This chapter will break down all the parts in the money engine and show you the one money tool that's completely unique to you: your goals.

The Moving Parts of Money (Money Tools)

To start getting a feel for the moving parts of money, it helps to have a handle on some simple definitions. Some of the terms you'll come across a lot in the money world are gross domestic product; inflation; interest; ROI; assets and liabilities; active, passive, and interest income; gross vs. net; and taxes.

Gross Domestic Product (GDP). Gross domestic product, or GDP, is the monetary value of all the finished goods and services produced within a country's borders in one year.

You can think about it this way: Imagine that you're in a classroom. The classroom has several desks, a bunch of chairs, a TV, a drawer full of pens, a teacher who gets a salary, and so on. All of these are worth a certain amount of money. If you were to add up the value of all those finished goods and services, that would be the gross domestic product for your classroom.

(Disclaimer: There's actually more to it than this

because a lot of different things factor into GDP, such as supply and demand. But this is the main idea.)

Now imagine that there are fifty classrooms in your school, and each of them has a different gross domestic product. For example, the room with all the weightlifting equipment might have a higher GDP than your room. This is what GDP looks like on a world scale. All the different countries are like all the different classrooms in your school.

Understanding GDP is important if your goal is to achieve wealth because it shows you how much money you're really going to have, long term.

Think of it like this. Imagine that you're going to take a vacation one year from now. You plan the flight, the hotel, the activities you want to do—everything. You know your budget and the total amount of money you're going to need when you get there. Then, one year from today, you go on your vacation, and when you get there, you discover something that kind of sucks.

Everything is more expensive than you thought it would be.

In one year, the cost of all those things you planned for went up. Suddenly you're stuck not knowing if you have enough to enjoy the vacation like you thought you would.

If you could have known that the price of everything was going to go up, would you have planned your finances better and taken into consideration that rise in the cost of your trip? Definitely. That's what GDP is really about.

Oh, and by the way, the name of that rise in cost over one year is . . .

Inflation. Inflation is the rate at which the general level of prices for goods and services (GDP) is rising.

What does that mean in practical terms?

It means that the cost of all the stuff you buy is going up on a yearly basis. Let's say you need to buy pens for your classroom, and the rate of inflation is 5 percent. The same box of pens that costs you $4.00 this year is going to cost you $4.20 next year because of inflation.

So really, the bottom line for you is that your twenty dollars buys less and less every single year. Here's a chart that shows how inflation works:

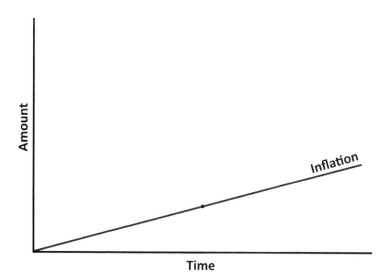

You want to find a way to grow your money at a percentage rate that's higher than the rate of inflation. Until your rate is better than inflation's, you're actually slowly losing money—and that makes it harder to gain true wealth and freedom.

Interest. Interest is the cost of borrowing money. Unless you're borrowing money from a friend or family member who's giving you a break, you have to pay back not only what you borrowed in the first place, but also some extra money on top of that—called interest.

Interest is generally calculated yearly. One term you'll hear a lot is "APR," which stands for annual percentage rate. So, for example, if you buy a car with 10 percent APR, you can use that to figure out how much interest you're paying on your car loan each month. All you have to do is divide that 10 percent by twelve months, and you can see that the loan will cost you an extra 0.83 percent in interest per month, on top of the money you have to pay back to begin with.

Wealthy people think about interest differently than everyone else.

Most people look at interest as bad. They do everything they can to avoid paying interest. However, wealthy people are okay with paying interest. Why? Because if they are paying interest, that means they are borrowing someone else's money in order to do something with it. And what are they going to do with it? Make more money. If they make enough money that they can pay the person or bank back and also make a profit from what they used it for, the interest doesn't even matter anymore, because they're still coming out ahead.

That's why being able to use other people's money—even with interest—is a very good thing. It's a critical part of becoming wealthy.

ROI (Return on Investment). ROI stands for return on investment. When you invest in something by buying it, your ROI measures how much money comes back to you as a result.

Here's the formula for ROI, calculated over one year:

$$\frac{Profits - Cost}{Cost} \ x \ 100 \ = \ ROI$$

Let's say you buy a shirt for $100, and a year later you sell it for $50. In this case, you collect $50, but your cost was $100. Plug these numbers into the ROI formula, and it turns out that your ROI on that shirt is actually *negative* 50 percent. That means investing in that shirt lost you 50 percent of your money over one year.

Now, let's say you buy a stock for $10 that goes up to $20 in value after one year. Plug these numbers into the same formula, and you see that investing in that stock gave you a 200 percent return on your money. Not bad.

The wealthiest people use the ROI formula to help them decide where to put their money based just on the numbers. It's not the only thing that matters when they pick their investments, but it is an important one.

Assets versus Liabilities. Assets are defined as "property owned by a person or company that is regarded as having value and that is available to meet debts, commitments, or legacies." In other words, assets are money coming in. Meanwhile, the definition of a liability is "an obligation that legally binds an individual or company to settle a debt." Liabilities are money going out.

Every time you use money to buy something, that thing you purchased is either an asset or a liability. It will keep bringing in money for you, or it will be a vehicle that sends money out, once or consistently, never to be seen again.

Think of it this way. Most sneakers that you buy lose value after you buy them. Those are liabilities. But if you buy a very rare pair of Jordans and hold on to them for a couple of years without wearing them, they go up in value, because the demand for them goes up and nobody has them. You can then sell those Jordans that you bought for $200 to someone else for $400. In this scenario, the Jordans are actually an asset.

Active, Passive, and Interest Income. You make money in three ways.

The first way is active income. This is money you have to work for. Your job is active income. Doing chores in exchange for your allowance is active income. Just think of it like it sounds: you have to do an "act" or "action" for money.

The second way is passive income. Passive income is something you buy that then makes you money on a monthly basis without additional work. If you buy a house and somebody pays you rent to live in it, the rent you collect from your tenant is passive income. We call passive income "mailbox money" because you don't have to go out and work for it; it just comes to you.

The third way to make money is interest income. With interest income, you lend money to someone else—another business, another person, whatever—and they then pay you back with interest. Not only do you get back what you gave them, but you also get a little extra based on the interest rate.

For example, say a friend of yours wanted to borrow $50. "Okay," you tell him, "I'll give you this $50, but when you pay me back I want $55." That extra $5 is your interest income, because you're getting paid 10 percent interest on the loan.

Are you starting to see how the more money you make from passive and interest income, the more freedom you have?

If not, no worries. We'll keep explaining it throughout the book. Stick with us. You'll get there.

Gross versus Net. When you make money, *gross* refers to the total amount that comes in. *Net* is the amount that you keep after deductions, expenses, or other costs.

Say you and two friends decide to split a pizza. You go to the pizza place and buy one whole pizza; that's your gross amount of pizza. Then you all start eating it, and you personally get only three slices. Those three slices are how much you netted out of that pizza.

When you have a job, the same thing happens with your paycheck. Your gross pay is the total amount that your employer is paying you. Your net pay is how much you actually get to keep and use, after taxes have been taken out.

Taxes. Taxes are a fee that the government charges you in order to finance government activities. When you make money, you pay taxes. At the end of the year, even if taxes have been taken out of your paycheck, you may still have to pay more. On the other hand, sometimes you'll get some of that money back.

The wealthiest people have learned how to do three things: make money, invest it, and save on taxes. Taxes are probably the most important thing that most people neglect to study and understand, financially. We'll talk more about taxes in chapter 6.

If you don't understand all of these terms perfectly yet, no worries. Learning the language of money is like learning any other language. The best way to learn it isn't usually by reading about it in school. It's by going to a country that speaks the language and living there. As soon as you get there, you start hearing certain phrases all the time, and even if you don't know what they mean at first, eventually you catch on and everything starts to make sense to you.

JP experienced this with a literal language.

In school, he studied Spanish for eight years but could barely speak it (his favorite phrase was "un poquito"). Then he moved to Costa Rica for six months, traveling, working, and enjoying life. After he got back to the States, he ran into a Spanish couple in San Diego who walked up to him on the street and asked him where the zoo was. He gave them directions and went on about his day. It was only a few minutes later that it hit him: he'd just had a full conversation in Spanish without even realizing it. He didn't even know when he'd gotten that competent. It just kind of happened while he was living in Costa Rica.

The same thing will happen with these money terms. You'll keep hearing them throughout the chapters ahead, and they might seem confusing for a while. But by the end of the book, you'll start to understand what all this means without even knowing it. Just stick it out until you get there.

The Missing Tool: What *You* Want

Understanding the moving parts of money can open a lot of paths. But before money can actually take you anywhere, you need to know exactly where you want to go.

You need specific goals for what you want your money to do for you.

Let's say you're trying to drive from New York to California, and you use Google Maps. Google Maps knows exactly where you're standing based on your current location. However, if you want it to show you how to get somewhere else, you have to plug in your destination. You can't just plug in "California," because that's not specific enough. You have to spell out the exact street address you want. Once you do that, Google Maps reverse engineers your route, starting with the end in mind, and tells you what the first turn is.

That's how money works, too. If you set specific goals for what you want, you can figure out exactly what it takes and how much money you need to reach your destination—and you can take the first steps in that direction.

How important are goals?

Harvard Business School actually did a ten-year study on this. In 1979, interviewers asked new graduates of the school's MBA program if they had set clear goals for themselves for after school was over. They found that 84 percent of students had no goals at all, 13 percent had goals but had failed to write them down, and only 3 percent had clear written goals and plans for how to accomplish them.

Then, in 1989, the interviewers followed up with those same students to see how well they were doing, financially. And what they found this time was that the 13 percent of students who had goals were earning twice as much as the 84 percent who had no goals at all, on average. Meanwhile, the 3 percent of students who had clear, written-down goals with a plan were earning an average of ten times as much as the other 97 percent of their graduating class. Pretty impressive.

"Okay," you might be thinking, "all of that sounds great—but what if I don't know what I want yet?"

If you don't know what you want, that's totally okay. What's not okay is not spending the time to think about it and figure it out. If you don't know what you want twenty years from now, then focus on goals that are closer. Where do you want to live after you graduate and move out? What would make you happy right now? Do you want your own apartment and your own transportation?

Every successful person starts with the end in mind. The sooner you pinpoint your goals, the sooner you can figure out how much they're going to cost—and the faster you can make them happen.

Got Purpose?

Ready to figure out your purpose? JP can walk you through it. Just check out the video at www.futurefortunebuilders.com. You can download our Future FortuneBuilders goal sheet there as well.

Talking Large Money

As Jay-Z says, "If we're not talking large money, what's the point?"

"Large money" can mean a lot of things to a lot of different people. Some feel they are living large when they have a big house, nice cars, and nice clothes and can go out to fancy restaurants whenever they want. Some feel they are living large when they have a smaller place but a loving family, or enough money to live quietly in the mountains, read books, and create pieces of art.

None of those ideas is wrong. But here's what it comes down to: whatever "living large" means for you, if you're not trying to live your life to the most extreme level of happiness you possibly can, then what's the point? If you want to strive for mediocrity, then you don't need this book.

But if you want to achieve your own version of lifestyle by design, no matter what that means, you're in the right place.

Because now you're starting to understand how to talk the talk of big money. That's a good start, but it's not the end of the line. Next, you need to learn how to walk the walk by actually starting to use these money tools we've just introduced you to in your own life.

Where do you apply them?

There are a few key turns on the road to true wealth and freedom that will get you to your destination fastest. The first one is getting crystal clear on where you're starting from by creating a budget and figuring out where you stand with something we call "the four buckets." We'll show you what you need to know about these in the next chapter.

Chapter 3

Your Budget and the Four Buckets

Wishful thinking is not *a strategy.*

—*Josh Shipp*

JP Does It All Wrong

When I finally learned how money grows, I got pretty excited. I set out to build up my assets column so that I could start to own my time and have real freedom. And at first it went pretty well. I started making more than six figures a year and studying investing, learning from Than Merrill and some other very wealthy people.

But even though I was making all this money, I still wasn't getting ahead as fast as I thought I should be. Somehow I just wasn't getting enough money into accounts where I could invest. Which got frustrating fast.

"How on earth is this not working?" I wondered. "Where is all the extra money that I should be able to invest right now?"

That was when I finally sat down and did a budget.

Everyone had always told me that making a budget was a good idea, and I totally agreed that it would be better. But I just didn't want to do it. "Yeah, I know it's a good idea . . . but I don't want to worry about budgeting. I'll just make more money and I won't spend too crazily, and I'll be fine," I figured.

Well, when I finally sat down and went through all my receipts and financial statements, my budget proved me wrong. Suddenly, I could see where every dollar I made was being spent. I had stopped spending on the big things, true—but I was losing $1,000 a month on a bunch of small things that I didn't even know I was spending money on. Things like coffee and snacks at the movies. One was a six-dollar-a-month subscription to something I'd forgotten about that was automatically being charged to my credit card. It really added up.

So I stopped buying all those little things, and I started putting that extra $1,000 into accounts that upped my assets column instead. Just like that, I was in control again. I knew where every last penny of my money was going. And that put me back in the driver's seat to financial freedom.

Money Trackers

When you start to make money, it goes to a number of different places. Some things you have to buy. Some things you want to buy.

Most people don't keep track of where their money goes. They spend it without even being aware of the big picture, so their finances are always in chaos. Money can't grow unless it's organized, so even if these people are making a lot of it, they never become truly wealthy.

Wealthy people, on the other hand, do things deliberately when it comes to money. Every time they decide to put their money somewhere, they do it with a clear intention—and that gives them maximum control. They understand that the more control they have over their money, the faster it can grow.

So how do you keep track of where your money is going at all times?

Two of the best tools out there for tracking exactly where your money is are budgets and something called "the four buckets."

Your Budget

A lot of people think they just need to make more money to get to the magic number of passive income over expenses.

And yes, making more is one part of it. But the other thing you can do is not spend as much.

This is where a budget can really help you out.

A budget is just a spreadsheet that tracks every dollar that you spend. It breaks down everything you buy into categories—living expenses, food, transportation, entertainment, etc.—and shows you how much money is going toward each thing on the list. It tells you where you're at right now financially: what's coming in and what's going out. And it shows you where you can spend less.

A lot of people think they know what they're spending their money on. But it's not until you actually put it on paper and stare it right in the face that you can see exactly where your money is going, down to the penny. And when you understand how money grows, every penny counts.

Making a budget shows the wealthy a ton of money that they can put into their assets column every month.

So how do you make a budget?

You can start with a simple Excel spreadsheet or download the one we use at www.futurefortunebuilders. com. Go online and check out templates. Then, all you have to do is fill in the blanks. Here's a breakdown of how much money should be going into each category if you want to achieve wealth at a steady, deliberate pace with a plan:

A GENERIC BUDGET PLAN, BY CATEGORY*		
Budget category	Typical budget percentage	Example with a $2,150 monthly net income
Housing	32%	$688
Auto	15%	$323
Food	15%	$323
Investing	10%	$215
Entertainment	7%	$151
Insurance	5%	$108
Clothing	5%	$108
Medical/dental	5%	$108
Miscellaneous	6%	$129

*Source credit: creditcards.com (slightly modified for an investing approach)

You may personally be able to save even more in some areas of this chart based on what you spend your money on. And where can you put that extra money? Wealthy people add as much of it into investing as soon as possible. That way, their overall passive income goes up faster, and eventually they can raise their take-home pay, along with how much they can spend in each of the other categories.

Your budget shows you exactly where you can spend less, so that more of the money you make can go toward building your passive income. Remember, every dollar counts.

The Four Buckets

Another great tool for keeping track of your money is the four buckets. A bucket is a place where you put your money. The four main buckets are spending, saving, investing, and giving back.

The Spending Bucket. The spending bucket is money going out. Your fixed expenses and any extra spending money for luxury things fall into this bucket.

The Saving Bucket. The saving bucket is for money that you're saving up for bigger purchases, such as holiday gifts, vacations, or a car. It's also for setting aside a little bit of extra money to cover a few months of expenses, in case something comes up and your active income stops unexpectedly. The saving bucket isn't designed to grow your money. That's what investing is for.

The Investing Bucket. The investing bucket is your assets. This is the bucket that gives you financial freedom—and the one that most people neglect for far too long, if they ever use it at all. Wealthy people put as much as they can in their investment buckets so that their money can grow.

The Giving Back Bucket. Giving back is an optional bucket. It's the next level of freedom and fulfillment. If you're someone who likes to get involved in helping others, this is the bucket you'll use to do that. We'll talk more about giving back in chapter 8.

Most of us make money, and if we don't spend it, it goes into one place: savings. We've been trained to do this ever since we were little and our parents gave us a piggy bank. From the get-go, we were told to put our money in one place and save it.

The wealthiest people don't do that.

The wealthiest people have to put some money in their spending bucket for their fixed expenses and some in their savings for larger purchases. When they build up enough wealth, they start to put money into the giving back bucket too. But they always keep their spending and saving buckets as low as possible. Why?

So that they can put as much as possible in the

investing bucket, where their money can make them even more money.

Eventually, all their income comes from investments. Do they still work? Yeah. But they work because they choose to, not because they have to. If you want to, you can do this, too.

Because you can't sign legal documents until you are eighteen years old, though, here is one of the first—if not the very first—things that you can do to get organized financially. Start separating your money into where you're going to put it in the four buckets now. Then, as soon as you turn eighteen, you can have your investing bucket up as high as possible and immediately make a strong move when you dive in. Even if you do nothing else but start to build the habit of separating your money into the buckets until you're eighteen, you will be a step ahead of most other people simply because you're preparing for the future.

One Step Ahead of the Future

When you know and track all the numbers, you take control of your money—and your future. You can reach the goals you set for yourself in chapter 2 because you see exactly what it takes to get there. If unexpected things come up, they don't faze you. You just sit down with your budget and your buckets, figure out where you can adjust the numbers, and let Google Maps recalculate your route.

You're one step ahead of the future, all the time. And that's a really good place to be.

So now you understand how a budget can help you save money, and you know what the four buckets are. But there's one particular area you need to learn more about if you want to earn true freedom: investing. That 10 percent in your budget today can and will (if you do certain things) turn into millions later. How do you actually use it? We'll break it down in chapter 4.

Chapter 4

INVEST IN YOUR FREEDOM

I prefer dangerous freedom over peaceful slavery.
　　　　　　　　　　　　　—Thomas Jefferson

JP Asks: Can We Play the Game Yet?

I'm in gym class at good ol' Winthrop High School, ten minutes from downtown Boston. We're about to start a new sport, one we'll be playing over the next week: kickball.

My teacher, Mr. Grimes, is standing in front of us with a rubber ball under his arm, and all I want is to grab it from him and get out on the field. I'm yearning for the chance to kick that thing. I just want to play.

Instead, Grimes spends that whole first day explaining *how* we're going to play. How to use the equipment, the rules, the teams—he just goes on and on.

Am I kind of bored and impatient? Yeah. But in retrospect, were all those rules completely necessary to prevent the chaos I'm sure Mr. Grimes wanted to avoid? Definitely.

You've been learning the rules of money. You've got all these tools—the terms, a budget, your goals—and maybe you feel like I did listening to Mr. Grimes drone on about kickball. You want to use this stuff. You want to apply it and start making lots of money.

If that's the case, I've got some good news for you. It's time to play ball. And the name of the game is investing.

How Investing Works

Investing is putting money somewhere with the expectation of getting either a profit or something of greater value in return. When you invest, your money goes to work for you instead of you going to work for your money. It goes out there and brings back more money, which is the passive income we've been talking about.

If you just save your money instead of investing it, the cost of things is going to go up faster than the interest you make on your savings (also known as inflation). What that means is that you're never going to make enough money through passive income to be free, and you'll always have to work.

That's why, if you want to be wealthy, investing is a must. Take a look at these charts that show how the poor, middle class, rich, and wealthy spend their money. What do you see?

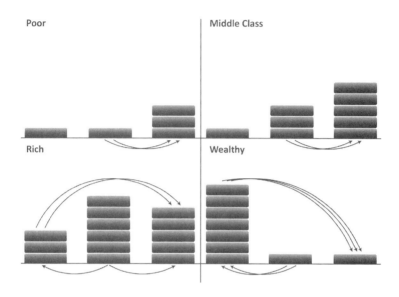

In the poor and middle-class charts, income comes in and goes right back out again through expenses and liabilities. Most people in the United States fall into these two categories. The only difference between the two, usually, is that the middle class just makes more money. They usually have very similar spending habits. With the rich, after their income passes through expenses and liabilities, they have enough left over to buy at least some assets so that they make more income.

Finally, you have the wealthy. And what the wealthiest people do that's different from everybody else is this: the line from assets to income is the first one they make. Which means that all of their income comes from what? Their assets.

But wait—how can the wealthy draw the first line from assets to income? Don't they have to make some money before they can even buy their assets?

Yes. Everyone, including the wealthy, starts with active income of some sort. It's just that the wealthy immediately use their extra money to buy assets that create passive income, so that they can control their time and do what they want as soon as possible.

They get to control their time and do what they want through the passive money they make from their investments. That's the key to their freedom—just like it can be the key to yours.

So how does investing work?

First things first: nothing is guaranteed. Anyone who tells you that an investment is guaranteed is lying to you. It's literally illegal to say so. There is always risk when you invest, and in fact most people don't invest at all because they think they might lose their money.

And they're right. They *could* lose their money. That's very possible. But here's the problem.

The reason they're likely to lose their money is because they haven't taken the time to study what to do with it before they invest. If you educate yourself on your investments, the level of risk involved goes down. Where do you start educating yourself?

You start just by understanding the different types of investments.

Types of Investments

There are all kinds of investments out there. Some of the most common ones are real estate, stocks, bonds, mutual funds, money market accounts, CDs, and interest income.

Here's our breakdown of each of these common investments based on our research and personal experience (and what we find are the most common ones you'll probably hear about).

Real estate. When we talk about real estate, we're not talking about buying and selling it. That's a little bit of a different beast. The kind of real estate investing that gives you passive income is rental properties.

Rental properties make you money in four ways:

1. Passive income. When you rent out a property, all the money left over after you use that rent check to pay the mortgage, taxes, and insurance on the property becomes positive cash flow—or passive income—for you.

2. Your renter pays off your mortgage. You borrow money from the bank to buy your rental property—but you don't pay off that debt yourself. Your renter pays it for you. After the mortgage is settled, you own a property that's worth thousands of dollars, and you didn't even have to pay for it yourself. This is a beautiful thing.

3. <u>Tax breaks</u>. When you invest in real estate, you also save money on taxes. The government gives you tax breaks for rental expenses, mortgage interest, property taxes, and many other things. You can also deduct the costs of buying and improving a rental property over time, which is called depreciation. Basically, this means that you won't be taxed on as much income in the first place, which saves you money. The bottom line is that houses have many different expenses. If you are aware, you can let the government know at the end of the year what some of those expenses were, and it will give you money back for owning property.

4. <u>Equity</u>. Finally, even though real estate goes through cycles, historically it goes up in value over time. A property you buy for $200,000 today might be worth $250,000 five years from now. That puts an extra $50,000 in equity in your pocket.

Keep in mind that rental properties don't always equal completely passive income. If you rent properties out to other people, you are responsible for picking up the rent, and if the tenants have any problems, then you have to either fix them or find someone else to fix them. That can add up to a lot of work.

Rental income becomes much more passive when you hire a property management company to manage all of that for you and you just collect the check. Whether you hire someone to do the legwork for you is up to your personal preference: you can make less money and do little to no work, or make a little more and do more work.

Stocks. A stock is a share in the ownership of a company. If you buy a share of stock in Google, it means you own a small piece of that company. You can make money on stocks in three ways. One, by buying them when they're priced low and then selling them for a higher price. Two, through dividends—sums of money that are paid regularly out of a company's profits or reserves. And three, through indexes, which are groups of stocks in a particular industry, such as technology or oil. An index invests in a group of companies. A single stock invests in just that—a single company.

Bonds. Bonds are like IOUs that the bank or the government owes you. You can loan your money to a company, a city, or the government in exchange for a bond, and it promises to pay you back in full with interest.

Mutual funds. A mutual fund is a company that gets people together and invests their money in a combination of things. Different mutual funds invest in different assets. Each investor owns shares in the fund and makes money from interest (like loans), from dividends (like stocks), or if the assets that the fund has invested in go up.

Money market accounts. Money market accounts are similar to savings accounts, except that they usually require a larger deposit. Once you have a certain amount of money in your money market account, your bank will give you a little bit more interest than you would earn in a regular savings account. You can access the money in this account at any time.

CDs. A CD (or certificate of deposit) is a certificate issued by a bank to a person who's willing to deposit money for a specific length of time. It's like saying, "Hey, I'll deposit this money in the bank and I won't touch it for X number of months or years." The longer you agree not to touch the money, the more interest your bank will pay.

Businesses. Businesses can be one of the best returns on investment there is, if you start the right one. You can use $100 of your money to start a business that could eventually grow into millions of dollars down the line. For example, you can pay $100 for the materials to open a lemonade stand

and make $200 at the end of the day. That's a 200 percent return on your money. Amazing ROI, right? But you could also spend that $100 on the lemonade stand and not make a dime.

Other investments. The investments we've covered are some of the most common ones, but they're not all of them. We don't have the space in this book to talk about every kind of investment out there. But when you're ready to go beyond this list, you can also look into things like annuities, currency, and gold—just to name a few.

Build Your Portfolio

Once you understand the different types of investments, you can decide which ones are right for you and start building something called a portfolio.

Your portfolio is just a collection of the different assets you've invested in. That doesn't mean you're going to invest in everything at once. In the beginning, you invest only in what you know. Pick one thing, learn everything you can about it, throw some money in the pot, and give it a shot. Then eventually, once you understand that one investment really well, you'll add another, and another, until you end up with a portfolio.

It's like being a pro basketball player. Usually, every off season, the best players work on their all-around game (consistently educating themselves and working on their craft). On top of that, they also try to add one new skill or significantly improve one new attribute every year. Then, once they've mastered it, they move on to something else the next year.

Why have a portfolio instead of just one type of investment?

We've said before that money is a game. Nowhere is that truer than with investing. There's always a chance you'll lose the game, and the longer you're in it, the more likely your chance of losing something at some point becomes. How much you prevent yourself from losing can be greatly affected by how well you structure your portfolio, because if you have a number of different investments, the risk of losing a lot of money goes down. Why?

Because you don't have all your eggs in one basket. It's like the pro basketball player. If, over time, you have developed enough skills and some days your jump shot is off, then you can drive to the hoop more or try to get more layups and free throws to compensate. If you have more than one skill, you can always find a way to win, instead of having just one skill to rely on that will wreck your whole game when you're having an off day.

As a real-life example, say you have five investments.

Two of them go down, and three go up. Obviously, how much each of them goes down or up makes a big difference, but you're usually more likely to win at the end of the day. The wealthiest people put their money into a lot of different assets and hope to profit from their investments as a whole every year.

How do you know which investments are right for you?

People have made money from all of the things we just talked about. Most of the time, the most successful ones get involved in multiple assets. The wealthiest people usually educate themselves on things with the best return on investment and go for those.

With investments in general, the safer the asset, the lower the payout usually is. In exchange for a little guarantee, you get a lot less interest. However, if you start investing early, even low-interest investments can go a long way toward winning you your freedom.

The Early Bird Gets the Money

Why start investing now, even if you don't have much money yet? Well, remember the whole compound interest thing we talked about in chapter 1? Here's how much your money grows in a savings account, compared with how much everything costs (the rate of inflation) over a few years:

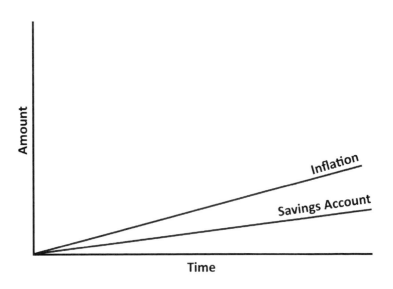

Now, here's how much your money grows compared with inflation if you invest it early:

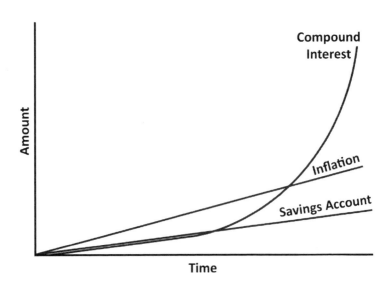

This goes back to the story of Ben and Arthur. If you invest just a little bit now, it will be the same as investing four times that much later. And it will buy you your freedom for the rest of your life.

Now, most things are going to be difficult to invest in before you're eighteen years old because you can't sign any documents as a minor. But if nothing else, you can learn as much as you can about your different investing options now, so that the second you turn eighteen you can immediately start investing. If you pile a lot of money into your investing bucket while you're waiting for your eighteenth birthday to get here, you'll have a lot more money than most to start with—and that compound interest line will take off big time.

More Education, Less Risk

There's a famous quote by Robert Kiyosaki that goes, "You don't get rich at work. You get rich doing your homework."

When it comes to investing, the more you educate yourself, the less risk you'll have. If you want to buy a stock, learn about how stocks work first. Figure out what the best stock investors are investing in that's working for them and ask them why it's working. Study what they're doing, understand it, and then do the same thing.

Now here's the thing: if you try to skip over all the stuff we talked about in the earlier chapters and just jump straight into investing, you will eventually give all of the money you might make back again. And that will happen over and over until you get the budgeting down.

But when you do decide to become a complete and educated financial expert, investing is the path that will take you in the direction you ultimately want to go.

The best part about investing is that it doesn't care who you are or what you look like. You don't have to come from a rich family or a poor family. It doesn't matter if you're black or white or Asian, or if you're a man or a woman. The only thing that matters is what you do with your money when you get it. If you put it right into assets, you're going to be wealthy. That's the bottom line.

When you understand investing, you can take a huge leap forward on the road to true freedom. But we're not done yet. We still haven't talked about one of the most important wealth strategies there is: leveraging other people's money, aka using credit. We'll show you how you can use leverage to stretch your money even further in the next chapter.

Chapter 5

Freedom through Credit

Everyone is entitled to his own opinion, but not his own facts.

—*Daniel Patrick Moynihan*

Playing with Fire

When we ask a group of high schoolers whether credit or, more specifically, credit cards are good or bad, they always give us the same answer: "Bad." Seriously—always. We're talking ninety-nine times out of a hundred.

But here's the thing: credit is the same as fire. Is fire good or bad? That depends on what you do with it. Are you cooking dinner or burning down a house? Is water good or bad? Same thing. It totally depends on how you use it.

Most people who think credit is bad are the ones who use it incorrectly or simply aren't educated enough to know how to use it in their favor. They use it to pay for things they don't have money for—inanimate things that give them no value and put them in debt.

But the wealthiest people love credit. They know how to use it to make money work for them, so it becomes a beneficial tool (not to mention all the things you actually need it for).

Credit can be an amazing tool for you on your road to financial freedom, too.

So what is credit, and why do we even have it?

What Is Credit?

Credit is what you could think of as your "financial résumé" as far as how likely you are to pay back the money you borrowed from some institution or individual. It's a vehicle for borrowing money, and it's a way to leverage other people's money. Basically, you get to use money that isn't yours for a certain period of time before you pay it back.

Credit is different from debit. The difference between a credit card and a debit card is that a debit card is specifically attached to your checking account, and a credit card is not. A credit card is someone else's money. A debit card is your money. There's usually very little benefit to using your debit card a lot—but there can be big benefits to using a credit card. So we're going to focus on credit in this chapter.

When you understand how credit works, your money can go further, faster.

The catch with credit is that, a lot of the time, it's one of those things that we usually don't understand until we've already screwed it up. And after we screw it up, it takes years to fix it again. In the meantime, you end up paying way more money on fees and interest than you need to, and it's harder to get the things you want—like buying your first house.

If you learn how to use credit intelligently from the beginning, though, that's a different story. You'll be able to use the bank's money to help *you* keep more money in your pocket and to increase your investments.

With good credit, you can do more with less money—and that will put you on the fast track to true wealth and financial freedom.

In this chapter, we'll show you how credit works and what you need it for. We'll also share a few tips you can use to build great credit.

How Credit Works

Good credit works in three ways.

One, it allows you to pay less interest for borrowing money.

Two, it allows you to leverage other people's money. Imagine if, instead of you borrowing money from your

parents and having to pay them back, your parents borrowed money from you and then paid you back with more
than you gave them. That's what leveraging other people's
money is like, except that instead of your parents, you're
dealing with the bank.

And three, when you commit to a payment (such as a
car payment or a cell phone bill), credit allows you to be
able to put as little money as possible down to start the
payment.

There are three types of credit:

Revolving credit. Revolving credit is credit that
never stops; it's continuously revolving. Every
month, as long as you're using it, there's always
a minimum payment. Credit cards are revolving
credit.

Ongoing credit. Ongoing credit is credit you
have to pay back in full. An example is charge
cards. The difference between a charge card and a
credit card is that, with charge cards, you usually
have to pay off the whole balance within thirty
or sixty days instead of just making a minimum
payment.

Installment loans. Installment loans are a type
of credit with an end date that you pay back in
installments over a period of time. Examples of

installment loans are student loans, mortgages, auto loans, and other personal loans.

When you start to use any type of credit, you get something called a credit score. A credit score, again, is your financial résumé. It measures how likely it is that you're going to pay back the person you're borrowing money from.

Think about your friends for a minute. Imagine that each of them wants to borrow fifty bucks from you. Now imagine that each of them has a number floating above his or her head: one of them has a 98 percent chance of paying you back, another has a 60 percent chance, another has a 12 percent chance, etc. Who are you going to give the fifty bucks to? Probably the ones with the higher numbers, right?

Well, this is ultimately what's happening when banks and lenders decide whether they want to lend you money. Instead of a number above your head, they look at your credit score. They take your social security number and look up anything that shows up on your report. The better that score (your credit history) is, the more likely you are to pay them back—and the better chance you have that they'll let you borrow money.

Your credit score is calculated by three big credit bureaus called Experian, Equifax, and TransUnion. Whenever you apply for credit, the place you're getting the loan from pulls your score from one of these three bureaus and decides whether to give you the loan based on what your score is.

The Five Things That Affect Your Credit Score

So what affects your credit score? There are five main things: payment history, amounts owed, length of history, new credit, and types of credit used.

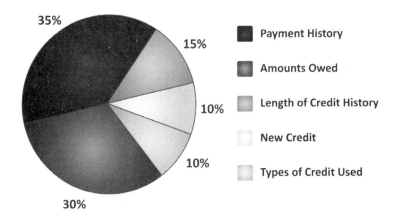

Source: myFICO.com

Payment history. The most significant part of your credit score is payment history. Have you made all of your payments? Have you ever missed a payment? Your payment history makes up 35 percent of your total score.

Amounts owed. Amounts owed is also called "debt-to-income" or "limit-to-balance." It looks at your balance versus your total credit limit—how much you've actually spent versus how much you can spend. If you keep your spending to less than 15 percent of the max limit, that helps your credit. Amounts owed makes up 30 percent of your credit score.

Length of history. This is how long you've had credit for. Anything under three years is really new, and anything under seven years is still pretty new. The longer you build up a good track record, the easier it is to get credit. Length of history is 15 percent of your total credit score.

New credit. This looks at whether you have any new open lines of credit. If so, how new are they? Do you have too many new lines of credit? This is another way to see if you're using credit well and makes up 10 percent of your total score.

Types of credit used. We talked about the three different types of credit. Credit companies want to see you using many types of credit, not just one or two. This accounts for the last 10 percent of your credit score.

As you build your credit, your credit score won't gradually go up in a straight line. It will look more like a squiggly line going up and down, with bigger swings at the beginning and smaller ones the longer you have it. If the line as a whole is headed up instead of down, you're in good shape.

Watch Your Step

Good credit can open a lot of doors for you. But you have to watch your step. It's easier to screw up your credit score than most people think—and once it's screwed up, it can take a long time to fix it.

The five things that will dock your credit score if you're not careful are missing a payment, canceling a card, sending out too many inquiries, not applying for new credit for a long time, and foreclosure, bankruptcy, or owing money to the IRS.

Missing a payment. If you miss one payment, it lasts seven years on your credit score. Even if it's the only payment you've ever missed, it can drop your score by up to 150 points (out of a possible total of 850).

Canceling a card. If you get a credit card and then cancel it, that usually hurts your score because it lowers your debt-to-income ratio. Think about it. If you cancel a card and then go out and ask someone to loan you money, the lender thinks, "Wait—you just gave back $5,000, and now you want to borrow money from me?" Lenders will be a little skeptical, and they may or may not give you money.

Too many inquiries. When you go to buy something big, like a car, you can apply for a loan in different places to shop for the best rate. If you have too many inquiries like these, the bank starts to think you're a risky person because you're asking for too much money too quickly. Inquiries can stay on your credit score for two years.

Haven't applied in a long time. It will also hurt your score and make it more difficult for you to get credit if you haven't applied for anything new in five to ten years. When you finally do go apply for credit, the lender thinks, "Where you have you been? What have you been doing that you suddenly need credit when you haven't needed it in five years?"

Foreclosure, bankruptcy, or owing the IRS. If you have a house and your house gets taken away from you because you can't make your payments, that foreclosure stays on your credit for seven to ten years. Same thing if you declare bankruptcy, or if you ever owe the IRS a lot of money (called tax liens).

Four Tips to Build Great Credit

Now you know what *not* to do when it comes to credit. But what about the flip side of the coin? How can you start building strong credit right away?

Here are four tips to build great credit.

Tip #1: Get a secured credit card. The second you turn eighteen, you can go to your bank and get what's called a secured credit card. What this means is that you'll give the bank $200, and it will give you a credit card with a $200 limit. You can use the secured credit card just like a regular credit card, paying it off every month. Then you can keep giving the bank more money to continue making your limit higher on your secured credit card, until one day—as long as you've used the card responsibly—the bank sends you a check for all the money you gave it and says, "Congratulations, we don't need this anymore. You now have a true credit card."

Tip #2: Apply for new lines of credit. If you ever want to buy a house, the lender will like to see at least three to five credit lines that you use responsibly. Remember, eventually you want a mix of revolving credit, ongoing credit, and installment loans. We try to apply for one or two new lines of credit every year.

Tip #3: Check your credit score. Most people don't ever look at their credit score. They never know what it is. Only one in five people checks his or her score every year. This is important because sometimes the credit bureaus can make mistakes with your score, and you need to be able to catch that and correct them. You can check your credit score at creditkarma.com or annualcreditreport. com.

Tip #4: Talk to the underwriters. When you apply for a loan, the application is accepted or rejected by someone called an underwriter. You can actually call the underwriters at your bank before you apply for a loan and ask them, "Hey, I'm thinking about applying for a credit card. Do you think I'll get approved?" or "I'm thinking of applying for a car loan soon. What do you guys see in people who get car loans that I can prepare for, so I have the best chance of getting approved when I apply?" If you do this, you'll be one step ahead of the game with your credit.

Remember, all of this is just an introduction. If you want to learn more about how to build really strong credit, you can check out the video of JP explaining exactly what he did to achieve a great score at www.futurefortunebuilders.com.

There's no perfect way to build credit. But just like any other part of money, once you understand the game, you can play it well and get yourself the best possible score at the end of the day.

The Power of Leverage

What wealthy people understand about credit is that it's not about the cost of money. It's about the accessibility of money.

You want to use credit only for things you have money for—unless you're going to use it for some sort of investing. If you have to pay 15 percent interest on your credit card, but you have the chance to make a 20 to 30 percent ROI (return on investment) on an investment, that's when you leverage or pay that minimum payment, including the interest. Then, once you make your money back from the investment, you pay the whole card off plus the interest—and you keep the profit.

This is just one more way that credit stretches your money to help it grow faster.

Leverage is a big part of building wealth. But just because you make money doesn't mean you get to keep it. In the next chapter, we'll talk about one of the most powerful ways to keep more money in your pocket: understanding taxes.

Chapter 6

FREEDOM FROM TAXES

The only thing that hurts more than having to pay an income tax is not having to pay an income tax.

—*Thomas Dewar*

Dave and the Tax Collectors

A good buddy of JP's, Dave, learned about taxes the hard way.

Not too long before the trouble started, Dave felt like he was really starting to understand money. "Okay, I get it now," he thought. "Don't spend too much, and start investing." Sure, he was a little behind on taxes, but he figured he'd just save some money and pay them off. He had great credit, he was studying investing, and he felt like that was enough.

Then one day, Dave was dropping his girlfriend off at her house when he got a phone call from his roommate. "Hey, Dave," his roomie said. "Somebody from the IRS came by the house for you."

Guys? Insider tip here. If someone from the IRS *physically comes to your house*, you're in trouble.

It turned out that the stuff Dave had been doing to catch up on his taxes wasn't enough. When he called this guy from the IRS, he said Dave needed to come up with $110,000 by next Friday. If Dave didn't, his credit would be wrecked—credit he'd built up for years and years.

"Okay," Dave told him, and then hung up. He needed $110,000 by next Friday. Wow.

Luckily, Dave had kind of known this was coming, so he had about $70,000 already saved for it. He ended up making it happen and coming up with the rest, and he gave the IRS the money in time to save his credit from annihilation. But in that moment, he realized that what he was doing with credit and investing wasn't enough.

He needed to understand taxes more than he did, as well.

The Truth about Taxes

A lot of people know more about the Kardashians than they do about what they're actually paying in taxes. They're just told, "You owe this much in taxes," and they pay it, or they get in a lot of trouble.

But the wealthiest people understand taxes. They know that the more they save on taxes, the more they can invest, and the more their money can grow.

So what are taxes, exactly?

Taxes are a percentage of your income that goes to fund the government, which uses them to do things such as fund roads, build schools, and pay the president's salary. As a free, contributing citizen of the United States, you pay taxes. It's just something you have to do.

Taxes aren't a bad thing so much as they're a necessary thing. And the wealthiest people are okay with paying taxes—but they're only okay with paying their fair share. If you don't understand how taxes work, a lot of times you'll pay way more than you have to.

Which is why the wealthy figure out ways to limit how much they have to pay in taxes—so they have more control over where their money goes. For the wealthiest people, the formula goes: make money, put it into assets for passive income, save on taxes.

Spending time learning about taxes is almost like active income. The more you study, the more money you get to keep in your pocket. There are some very specific, totally legal, government-approved strategies out there that can cut down the amount you have to pay on taxes so you can put that money toward building your future instead.

With taxes, it's not about how much you make. It's about how much you keep. And when you understand how taxes work, you'll keep a lot of money. In this chapter, we'll show you the basics about how taxes work and how you can save as much money on them as possible.

How Taxes Work

So how do taxes work? What kinds of taxes do you have to pay? And when do you actually need to file them?

Generally, there are two types of taxes you have to pay: federal income tax and state income tax. Everyone in the country pays the federal income tax, and most people pay the state income tax, too. There are seven US states that don't have any state income tax: Alaska, Florida, Nevada, South Dakota, Texas, Washington, and Wyoming. If you live in New Hampshire or Tennessee, you almost don't have to worry about a state income tax; you just have to pay taxes to the state on dividends and the income you make from investments.

As for when you need to file your federal taxes, that depends on how much money you make, and the numbers can change every year.*

If you work for someone else, are single, and are under sixty-five years old, you have to file your taxes when you make $10,350 a year or more, as of 2016. To file them, you're going to get a W-2 from your employer that looks like this:

---

*   The numbers throughout this chapter are correct as of 2017 and subject to change.

22222	Void ☐	a Employee's social security number	For Official Use Only ▶ OMB No. 1545-0008		
b Employer identification number (EIN)				1 Wages, tips, other compensation	2 Federal income tax withheld
c Employer's name, address, and ZIP code				3 Social security wages	4 Social security tax withheld
				5 Medicare wages and tips	6 Medicare tax withheld
				7 Social security tips	8 Allocated tips
d Control number				9 Verification code	10 Dependent care benefits
e Employer's first name and initial	Last name		Suff.	11 Nonqualified plans	12a See instructions for box 12
				13 Statutory employee / Retirement plan / Third party sick pay	12b
				14 Other	12c
					12d
f Employee's address and ZIP code					
15 State	Employer's state ID number	16 State wages, tips, etc	17 State income tax	18 Local wages, tips, etc	19 Local income tax	20 Locality name

W-2 Wage and Tax Statement **2017**

Form

Copy A For Social Security Administration — Send this entire page with
Form W-3 to the Social Security Administration; photocopies are **not** acceptable.

Department of the Treasury—Internal Revenue Service
For Privacy Act and Paperwork Reduction
Act Notice, see the separate instructions.

Cat. No. 10134D

Do Not Cut, Fold, or Staple Forms on This Page

Even if you make less than $10,350 from your job, you may want to file a tax return anyway, because you may get a refund if your employer withheld taxes from your paychecks and you didn't make too much.

Meanwhile, if you're self-employed, you have to file your taxes if you make more than $400 in a calendar year.

The percentage you pay in taxes is based on something called tax brackets. A tax bracket is a range of incomes that are subject to the same income tax rate. Usually, lower tax brackets have relatively low income tax rates while higher brackets have larger ones. Here's a chart of income tax brackets in the United States as of 2015:

2016 Federal Income Tax Brackets

Tax Rate	Single	Married, filling jointly	Married, filling separately	Head of Household
10%	$0 to $9,275	$0 to $18,550	$0 to $9,275	$0 to $13,250
15%	$9,276 to $37,650	$18,550 to $75,300	$9,275 to $37,650	$13,250 to $50,400
25%	$37,650 to $91,150	$75,300 to $151,900	$37,650 to $75,950	$50,400 to $130,150
28%	$91,150 to $190,150	$151,900 to $231,450	$75,950 to $115,725	$130,150 to $210,800
33%	$190,150 to $413,350	$231,450 to $413,350	$115,725 to $206,675	$210,800 to $413,350
35%	$413,350 to $415,050	$413,350 to $466,950	$206,675 to $233,475	$413,350 to $441,000
39.6%	$415,050 or more	$466,950 or more	$233,475 or more	$441,000 or more

Ways to Save Money on Taxes

You can save money on taxes whether you're self-employed or work for someone else.

If you're self-employed—which means you work for yourself and own a business—you have a lot more tax breaks. The main way you get them is through write-offs.

Write-offs are expenses relating to your business that can be deducted from your taxable income on your tax returns. For example, say you make $100,000 a year, and you have $10,000 in write-offs. In that case, you pay taxes on only $90,000 in income, instead of the full $100,000.

If you work for someone else, you have very few tax

breaks. But you do have another way to save money on taxes: retirement accounts.

Retirement accounts are one of the best ways to help your money grow tax-free. If you make investments in your personal name, and they grow, you have to pay taxes on that. With retirement accounts, you don't escape taxes completely, but you can save a lot of money on them. The most common types of retirement accounts are 401(k)s, IRAs, and Roth IRAs.

401(k)s. A 401(k) is a retirement savings plan sponsored by your employer. With 401(k)s, you give your money not to your employer, but to a company that your employer sponsors. The company then invests your money for you, usually in things such as stocks, bonds, and mutual funds. You generally have little to no control over what the company invests in. When you put a piece of your paycheck in your 401(k), you don't pay taxes on it up front, but you do pay taxes on it when you take the money out at age 59½ or older.

IRAs. Like 401(k)s, IRAs are retirement plans set up by your employer. IRA stands for individual retirement account. IRAs are designed to help you save for retirement, and they offer a lot of tax advantages. Just as with 401(k)s, you don't get taxed on the money you put into them at first, and the money is taxed when you take it out of the account later. If you take it out before you're 59½, you're charged a 10 percent penalty on the money.

With IRAs, there's a limit to how much money you can add to it per year. As of 2017, the maximum amount was $5,500. Unlike 401(k)s, with IRAs you have a little more control over the kinds of assets your money is invested in while it's in the account. To put money into an IRA, you have to be younger than 70½ years old.

Roth IRAs. Roth IRAs are a type of IRA with a few unique provisions. The biggest one is that you pay taxes on the money that you put into your Roth up front. Then, when you take the money out later, you don't pay taxes on it—even the money you make on investments from that account.

What's great about Roth IRAs is something called growth versus compensation. As with regular IRAs, there's a limited amount of money you can put into a Roth each year—$5,500 as of 2017. However, that money can have unlimited growth. Let's say you put $5,500 into your Roth IRA for four years, and then you take that $22,000 and invest it in a rental property. Your rental property pays you $500 every month. That $500 goes into your Roth without being taxed. And guess what? Because you paid your taxes up front, if that money grows to $5 million by the time you take it out when you're 59½, you don't have to pay taxes on it.

There's no age restriction when it comes to contributing to a Roth IRA, but there are income limits. As of 2017, as a single person, you cannot contribute to a Roth IRA if your taxable income is $118,000 or more. As with traditional IRAs, if you take money out of your Roth before you're 59½, you pay a 10 percent penalty on the money.

Tax Freedom

Is there more to learn about taxes? Absolutely. There are so many ways to save money on taxes, especially if you start a business. But even these two simple things—write-offs and retirement accounts—can save you a ton of money if you understand them. The more money you keep, the more you can put into your investing bucket, and the closer you get to true wealth and freedom.

Have you saved as much money as you can once you understand taxes? Not quite—especially if you're planning to go to college after high school. In the next chapter, we'll show you how you can save on one of the biggest expenses of your life: student loans.

Chapter 7

FREEDOM FROM STUDENT LOANS

If you think education is expensive, try ignorance.

—*Derek Bok*

The Money Pit

Sarah took out three student loans for college, and she was on top of them. No way was she going to let the interest on those things eat her alive for ten whole years (the full term of the loans). She paid all of them off early, three years after she got out of school. Smart move, right?

Not so much, actually.

Because it turned out that even though Sarah paid off her loans early, she missed the fine print. Guess what that fine print said?

It said that even if she paid the loans off early, she had to cough up the same amount of interest that she would have had to pay over the full ten years anyway—a cool $23 grand.

But what's the difference, right? Pay it off now, pay it off later: Sarah would've lost $23,000 either way, in the end. Wouldn't she?

Sure. Unless you understand compound interest.

Remember the story of Ben and Arthur, from chapter 1? You know how Ben invested $16,000 and made way more money in the end than Arthur, who started investing with $78,000, eight years after Ben?

Yeah, same story with Sarah. She could have invested most of that $23,000 instead of shoveling it all into the pit of her student loans right away. And that could have made her thousands of dollars that she'll never see. Money she could have used to do what she loves—travel the world.

Sarah realized her mistake too late. But this doesn't have to happen to you. Not if you understand student loans *before* you sign on the dotted line.

The Price of Education

Hey, listen, we're not here to tell you that you should or shouldn't go to college. That's a decision you need to make for yourself, based on your goals.

With that said, a lot of high schoolers do decide to go to college after high school—and college can be expensive. Many of us might not have the money to pay for it. That's where student loans come in.

Student loans are loans designed specifically for school.

They help you pay for the fees involved in your postsecondary education—things like tuition, books, supplies, and living expenses.

But student loans can be a money pit if you don't understand them. A lot of people sign up for them and find out later that the interest rate was more than they thought, or that they can't use the money to pay for just anything. Sometimes they get stuck paying thousands of dollars more in unexpected penalties and fees—money that could have gone toward investing and winning financial freedom.

A lot of times in high school, we make the decision to get a student loan just because we're told to. But you don't want to mindlessly follow the crowd and get just any student loan. You want it to be a conscious decision, and you want the loan you choose to be the right student loan for you so that you can plan for the expense ahead of time and stay in control of your money.

This chapter will break down the different kinds of student loans, so that you can be prepared to pay them back, save as much as possible on your education, and plan the next few years of your life.

Fill Out the FAFSA

First things first: fill out the FAFSA.

You don't want to pay money if you don't have to. The FAFSA is the Free Application for Federal Student Aid.

You can fill this out to find out if you are eligible for federal loans, grants, or work-study programs.

Don't just assume that you won't qualify for FAFSA aid. Some federal loans are need based, but others don't care what your family income is. Plus, sometimes schools require your FAFSA to be on file.

Federal financial aid is given on a first come, first served basis, so the sooner you fill this out, the better. Typically, you can start the process in January. And don't just do it once: filling out the FAFSA should be a staple every year you are looking to apply for loans. You can find the FAFSA application at www.fafsa.ed.gov.

Types of Student Loans

The FAFSA helps you with federal student loans, which will help you find most of your options for financial aid. But the FAFSA isn't the only way to fund your education.

You can also look into state and private loans.

A few different kinds of loans are available to you. Here is a quick breakdown of the different types, with their approximate interest rates and fees.[*]

---

[*]   Interest rates and fees are subject to change yearly. The rates and fees listed here are current as of 2017. Rates were taken from www.studentaid.ed.gov.

Direct Subsidized Loans *(Undergraduate).* Because this is a loan for students who show that they need financial help, you will get better terms on this loan than you will on some others. The US Department of Education will pay the interest on the loan for at least the first six months that you're in school (and even six months after you graduate, if there is a deferment period), and the school will determine how much money you can receive.

- Interest rate: 3.76%
- Loan fee: 1.068%

Direct Unsubsidized Loans *(Undergraduate).* Your financial situation does not matter with this loan. The interest rate is different, depending on whether you're a graduate or undergraduate student.

Undergraduate:
- Interest rate: 3.76%
- Loan fee: 1.068%

Graduate:
- Interest rate: 5.31%
- Loan fee: 1.068%

PLUS Loans. PLUS loans are for students who want to pursue graduate or professional degrees. The parents of dependent undergraduate students can also apply for this kind of loan. You can't have a bad credit history when you apply for a PLUS loan, but if you apply what you learned in chapter 5 about credit, you should be in good shape.

- <u>Interest rate</u>: 6.31%
- <u>Loan fee</u>: 4.276%

Perkins Loans. Perkins loans are for graduate or undergraduate students who show what is considered to be "exceptional" financial need. Your school will be the lender and will determine how much money you will be able to get. Not all schools offer Perkins loans.

- <u>Interest rate</u>: 5%
- <u>Loan fee</u>: 0

You may also want to take the time to look into individual state loans and private loans. These loans can be awarded depending on your credit and where you live, and their rates can vary greatly.

Other Ways to Pay for College

Loans aren't always the only way to pay for college. You can also look into grants, scholarships, and work-study programs.

> *Grants and Scholarships.* Grants and scholarships are a great way to get funding for school because you don't have to pay them back. You can receive grants from the federal government, as well as from your state and various private institutions. People give out grants and scholarships for a lot of different reasons. They can be need based, merit based, or based upon your ethnicity or gender. Some are also given to students who have disabilities. If you look into which grants and scholarships are available to you early enough, you can start to work toward qualifying for them right from freshman year.

> *Work-Study Programs.* If your school offers it, you can get a job through the school to help pay for your tuition. This is called a work-study program.

The Four Steps

After you decide on a loan that's right for you, you don't want to just take it out and forget about it. If you do, it'll probably come back to bite you. Here are four steps you can take to stay on top of your student loans until the day you pay them off for good.

Step 1: Know your loans. Keep track of the lender, balance, and repayment status for each of your loans. An easy way to do this is to just keep all that information in a spreadsheet. If you do this, you won't get blindsided when the payments kick in, and you can build those payments into your budget so that you have as much control over your money as possible.

Step 2: Know your grace period. A grace period tells you how long you have until you need to actually start paying back your loans. Different loans have different grace periods, and sometimes you can push the grace period off. It's important to know your grace period because if you don't, you could miss your first payment by accident—and that will hurt your credit.

Step 3: Know your options. Once you do have to start paying back your loans, you have options. A lot of loans are broken down into ten-year payment plans, and sometimes you can change that if you need to. Just be aware that the longer you take to pay back your loans, the more it will cost you in interest. Sometimes you can also prepay loans. If you have multiple loans, you can consolidate them down into one. You can qualify for income-based repayment plans, and some professions qualify for income forgiveness after ten years of payments—which means that if you make payments for the first ten years, the lender may forgive the rest of it.

Step 4: Don't ignore them. Make sure you don't ignore your student loans. If you default on them, two things will happen. First, it will hurt your credit. And second, a lot of times the lender will add extra fees and interest—which will make the loans even more expensive. If you don't pay them, the lender can also decide to make your total balance due immediately, and it could even get to the point where they take money straight from your paycheck or from your tax refund to pay back the loans.

By the way, in most cases, you can also deduct a good chunk of interest paid on your student loans—up to $2,500 for the year 2017—from your taxes. Just thought you'd like to know.

Beyond Student Loans

If all these student loan options are freaking you out a little, don't panic. There are other ways to pay for college. You can look into things like scholarships, grants, and sometimes even work-study programs to help you get college paid for.

But if you do need a student loan, you don't need to panic, either. As long as you do your homework, know the facts, and follow the four steps, you'll come out on top in the end—and paying back your loans will just be one more fully mapped route on your way to financial freedom.

In the next chapter, we'll show you one of the most exciting and fulfilling things you can do once you reach Destination Freedom: giving back.

Chapter 8

THE FREEDOM TO GIVE BACK

*Every single day, in every walk of life, ordinary people
do extraordinary things. Ordinary people accomplish
extraordinary things.*

—Reverend Bob Richards

JP's Good Karma

In San Diego, where I live, there are a lot of homeless
people. Heck, if I were going to be homeless, I'd do it
in San Diego because of the weather. But at one point, I
noticed that some people were critical of the less fortunate.
Even some of my friends made comments like "They
should just get a job" or "You could figure it out if you
wanted to."

That bothered me because I have a hard time criti-
cizing someone unless I've walked a mile in that person's
shoes. I am also not someone who dwells on problems. If
I see a problem, I don't sit there and complain; I try to fix

it. In my opinion, you have no right to complain about a problem unless you've actually looked into it and tried to fix it first.

So I decided to hold an event to help the homeless.

I put together a $10,000 charity event for homeless people just because I personally wanted to give back. We brought in people to cut their hair, vendors they could talk to about applying for housing, a veteran's trailer where veterans could get benefits, and hot showers. About a hundred homeless people came through our clinic that day, and all of them left in better shape than they came. We even helped one woman get a birth certificate, which pretty much gave her a new lease on life.

After it was over, I remember sitting on my couch and literally basking in the feeling of fulfillment. I was exhausted from the day and all the months of planning leading up to it, but I had never felt such inner happiness. I felt like I had made a dent in the world that day. I'd changed it in a small way, and it was a better place because I was here.

And the rewards didn't stop there. After that event, I noticed that good things started happening to me as a result of it. Opportunities to move up at work suddenly appeared. I got all these inspirational and giving-back awards that made people want to help and work with me. My multimillionaire mentors told me that I inspired *them*. It was a really cool feeling.

For me, giving back created what some people call good karma. And I'm not the only one.

Giving Back: The Ultimate Freedom

When you do something amazing, you feel good. But when you do something amazing for others and then *they* feel amazing, it's a whole new level of fulfillment.

That's what giving back is all about. In its simplest form, giving back means helping others. It's being part of a greater cause—something that improves the world around you.

Gaining wealth and freedom without giving back is like getting front-row tickets to see your favorite musical artist, but then turning down the chance to meet the band in person after the show. If you don't give back, will it hurt you? No, probably not. But you'll be missing out on one of the greatest highs in life, which is the fulfillment you feel when you help others become a better version of themselves.

Giving back is about understanding that, with your education, you can help a lot of people. When you give back, you reach a new level of freedom. Not only have you earned freedom for yourself, but you also have the ability to share it with others.

The other thing about giving back is that when you help other people, good things tend to come back to you tenfold. As JP says, "Karma is a great thing." The more you help people get what they want, the more you'll seem to find yourself getting what you want. It's a win-win any way you look at it.

This chapter will let you in on the practical benefit of giving back and show you how one good deed on your part can start a domino effect of inspiration.

Give Back, Get Back

Giving back is pretty amazing just in itself because of how it makes you feel. But it gets even better: when you give back, the government will actually allow you to keep more of your money through tax breaks.

You can look at it this way: bottom line, you have to give money to the government in taxes. But if you make charitable donations, those come off the top of your taxable income. So what that means is that instead of giving your money to the government and letting it decide what to do with it, you can say, "I want to do something great with this money," and put it toward a cause that you really love.

Now, the cause you donate to has to be qualified in order for you to get a tax deduction. Qualified organizations include nonprofit groups that are religious, charitable, educational, scientific, or literary, as well as groups that work to prevent cruelty to children and animals.

A lot of wealthy people choose to give back (and get

back) instead of just paying their taxes to the government. After all, you're going to have to cough up the money either way. Why not put it toward something you care about?

The Domino Effect

People always say, "What can I do to make the world better? I'm only one person." Right?

Wrong. One person can make a difference in the world. It happens through a domino effect called inspiration.

Inspiration is not about telling people what to do. People get inspired by you doing something you're passionate about at a high level. One thing leads to another, and sometimes the results are huge.

A great example of this is a man named Edwin Land. If we asked you who Edwin Land was, you'd probably have no idea. Edwin Land was the creator of the Polaroid. His philosophy was that he wanted his business to be the intersection between art and science. Guess who got inspired by that philosophy? A man by the name of Steve Jobs—the founder of Apple.

Now, would you consider Steve Jobs somebody who changed the world? Absolutely.

But Edwin Land never told Steve Jobs to do anything. Edwin Land just did business the way he felt was right and unique. Somebody else saw that and changed the world in a big way because of it.

There are countless stories like this one in the world. Than himself started a nonprofit with his wife, Cindy, called the Equal Footing Foundation, which helps fund sports programs for underprivileged children. Likewise, FortuneBuilders has organized hundreds of charitable giving events over the years. You can check out the website www.fortunebuildersgives.com to see many of the things we ourselves do to give back.

When you choose to give back, you can be an inspiration for others. Even if you help only one person, animal, or cause, you might do something that inspires somebody else—and set in motion a domino effect of inspiration that's all your own.

In the last chapter, we'll share the key to turning your dreams of wealth and freedom into reality.

Chapter 9

FREEDOM FOR THE REST OF YOUR LIFE

The saddest thing in life is wasted talent.

—A Bronx Tale

JP's High School Graduation (That Almost Didn't Happen)

I almost didn't graduate high school.

Fifteen-year-old me had this philosophy: if you can't tell me how high school relates to the real world, then I'm not going to do it. I'll figure it out on my own. My plan was that I was going to do just enough to graduate—and that was it. I almost never did homework. If anyone asked me why, my response was "I just didn't want to."

Then, during the third quarter of my senior year, I got called down to the office to see my guidance counselor, Miss Thaxton. "JP," she told me, "you're not going to graduate. We need to pick out your classes for next year."

I was shell-shocked. "What?" I blurted. "That's not

possible!" Miss Thaxton assured me that it was. "No way,"
I said. "Tell me it's mathematically impossible for me to
graduate, and I'll believe you."

"Well," Miss Thaxton said, "it's not *mathematically*
impossible . . ." She showed me what grades I needed to
get to graduate. I had to get straight A's in every class but
gym, and I had to get the same grade on every single final.
She wrote it all down on a piece of paper.

Okay, there's an opening, I thought. I took the paper off
her desk and said very casually, "Hey, Miss Thaxton, don't
worry. I've got this."

Miss Thaxton looked at me with this face I'll never
forget—befuddled, but also kind of curious. Like she was
thinking, *I doubt it, because you haven't done it for 3¾
years . . . but let's see.*

When I got back to class, I had a newfound reason
to do schoolwork—a zest for it, even. Partially, I just
wanted to prove that I could play ball—that I could do it
if I wanted to. The other part of it was that, well, I didn't
want to stay back. *I'm going to do this*, I thought. *I'm going
to do everything that I know I need to do, and I'm going to
graduate.*

And that's exactly what I did.

My teachers didn't give me an inch, but I did it anyway.
I worked hard, and I aced every school assignment, every
piece of homework, every final. On the day of graduation,
I had to go into the guidance counselor's office again to

see if I was graduating or not. I literally walked into Miss Thaxton's office before the ceremony and said, "Did I make it? Am I graduating?"

She could barely get the words out. "Yeah," she said. "I still don't believe that it happened, but yeah, you are."

"Cool," I said. "Can I get a cap and gown?"

My cap and gown were one size too big, but I put them on and ran down to join the rest of my graduating class. Most kids who crossed the stage to get their diplomas that day got the little golf claps from the audience. But when they called my name, my friends ripped up a wild cheer of hooting and applause.

That fourth quarter of my senior year was when I realized a big piece of the puzzle. Because all I did that quarter was what I knew I was supposed to do. I studied when I had tests. When I had projects, I did them better than I needed to do them. I got straight A's that quarter because, bottom line, I went home after school and did my homework.

And just like that, I got my answer to "What does homework have to do with real life?" Because what you're really learning in high school with homework is how to set time aside to work on getting better—and the most successful people always put time aside to get better.

That's what homework has to do with the real world.

The Doers and the Dreamers

You know this drill.

All high school athletes get off-season workouts. There is always summer reading to prepare you for the next school year. If you take an honest look in the mirror and ask yourself, "Will I be a better player this upcoming season if I do the entire off-season workout routine, including all the optional trainings? Even do more than I am required to do?" or "Will I be more prepared for that class if I read the recommended books going in? Will this little sacrifice now make my life easier later?" you know the answer.

Here's the thing, though. Just knowing the answer isn't enough.

The biggest difference between the people who are successful and the people who aren't is this: Pretty much everyone knows what to do. But the successful people are the ones who actually do it.

Just by reading this book, you've probably done more "homework" on money than most people ever have. And you can pat yourself on the back for that, but here's the truth: it doesn't mean anything until you implement it. The most successful people are not satisfied until they have the results they want. This book is just a stepping stone in the direction of wealth and freedom. We gave you the information you need to know about how money works.

But the people who want it do the homework.

To actually make all this stuff work for you, you're going to have to keep studying it. Which investments are you going to try? What strategies are you going to use to build your credit? You know what to do. The question is, will you do it?

This is where we separate the doers from the dreamers. You've got dreams. You can see that they're possible. To get to them, you have to go walk the walk. Go out and make it happen. Start with one thing, if that's all you can do. Then add one more. And then maybe one more, until you've reached the life you've always wanted.

Success is work. Anyone who tells you otherwise is wrong. And we can promise you this: on the road to wealth and freedom, you're going to fail. You won't always win with investing. But if you're afraid to fail, you'll never achieve the things you want. So go for it. Because even if you fail, you'll learn what to do better next time.

In fact, here's a secret: now that you understand how money works, failure can't hurt you. Not really. Lots of wealthy people have had financially tough periods in their lives, but that doesn't concern them. Why? Because if they lose money on an investment, they learn from their mistakes, and they don't repeat them. Once you understand the process of obtaining money, you can have true security for the rest of your life—just like they do.

Homework isn't a negative thing. It's a positive thing. Because homework doesn't just make you rich; it makes you wealthy. It gives you freedom. And it's worth every minute you put into it.

The Long Road and the Fast Track

Okay, next question: If you're going to do homework, do you want to take the long road? Or do you want to get on the fast track?

Because you can go and try to do all of this on your own. That's definitely an option. But the most successful people go a different route.

The most successful people choose "deliberate practice."

What's deliberate practice? Why is it better than regular practice?

Think of it this way. Let's say you want to be a boxing all-star. You can get in the ring on your own and drill boxing moves for five hours—and you'll get better. That's regular practice. But now let's say you had Muhammad Ali standing next to you and watching your every move while you practiced. Every time you took a punch, he'd correct your form, saying, "No, do it this way."

Do you think you'd get better faster than just climbing into the ring alone and swinging away?

That's deliberate practice.

Instead of spending five hours practicing what you think you should practice, you can spend all that time practicing the *exact thing* that you really need to practice.

The most successful people choose deliberate practice because it shortens the learning curve. It puts them on the fast track to what they really want.

But how do you find your own Muhammad Ali?

Old Wheel, New Rims

Money is a big subject. You can always go deeper, always learn more about it. That's why, if you want to travel the road to wealth as quickly and smoothly as possible, you want to find a mentor—someone else who already has what you want.

Mentors aren't there to tell you what to do. They're there because they have the one thing you need more than anything else when you're working toward building wealth: knowledge. When it comes to money, more knowledge equals less risk. Mentors can answer the questions you have about money, because they've experienced everything you want to do with it for themselves. They share those experiences with you. From there, you take that information and use it to make decisions that are right for you, personally.

Remember, just because you aren't reinventing the wheel doesn't mean you can't put your own rims on it.

The more you're around people who have what you want, the more likely you are to get it. Find those people, and do whatever you can to be around them. Work for them. Read about them. Pay them if you have to, because the school of hard knocks costs a lot more money than any other school you'll ever go to.

Even if you look around you and don't see anyone who has what you want, you don't have to do this alone. We've been down the road to wealth, and we are here for you. We can be your first money mentors. If you don't know where to start, visit us at www.futurefortunebuilders.com for tons of free resources and ideas.

You can even ask JP to come out and talk to you and your school. He does camps all around the country, where you'll be in a live environment learning this information, surrounded by other high schoolers who want the same things and think the same way you do. People your age who want to make a difference, live free, and help others. People who want to make life happen instead of waiting around for a free ride.

Look, it's like JP said in the introduction: We didn't just write this book for you. We wrote it for our fifteen-year-old selves. And those guys would've wanted more than just words. They would've thought, "It would be amazing to have some tools that would actually let us start using this information, so that we can make some money as fast as possible."

That's literally why we created Future FortuneBuilders: so that we could put everything we know about money into a time capsule and send it back to ourselves, and you, with a note that says, "Hey, enjoy yourself. It's all possible."

So come to the Future FortuneBuilders camps. Use the bonuses we've created for you. Go online and check out the information we've pulled together at www.future-fortunebuilders.com. If you want to make sure you've got quality mentors and coaches to teach you how this stuff works, we're here for you. This knowledge has been tested by people who have done hundreds of millions of dollars in business.

And once you get started learning about money, stick with it. The most successful people know that consistency matters. Small actions made every single day over time add up—just like compound interest. You can't be in the gym with Muhammad Ali for just one day and expect to come out of there a world champion.

But you *can* become a champion. You *can* practice money, practice success, and practice being the best version of yourself.

Surround yourself with people and resources that will help you do those things. Just remember that everything starts with you.

The Magnifying Glass

When you're born, you're dropped into a lottery. Who you've been up until this point, who you've had as parents, your financial situation—you didn't have a say in the matter. Right?

But now that you're in high school, things are different. Now, you start to have a say.

When you start putting the strategies in this book into action and telling people about it, you need to understand one thing: Everyone is going to have an opinion about it. Everyone is going to start telling you what they think you should do with your money.

Here's our recommendation: Don't worry about what those people say or think. Do your own research, and make your own educated decisions on what you should do. At the end of the day, there's only one person you're going to have to answer to when it comes to building your future: you.

If anybody's told you that you can't do something, we're telling you right now they're wrong. You can do anything you want. And when you understand money, you will be able to prove it that much faster.

Remember that who you are without money is who you'll be with it. If you're a bad person without money, you'll be an even worse person with money. But if you're a genuinely good human being, and you earn $10 million, we'd be willing to bet you'd do something good with it.

Money doesn't make you good or bad. It just puts a magnifying glass on who you are. Having more money is not going to change you. It will just give you a lot more freedom and time to do the things that you already love to do.

We've said it before, but it bears repeating: wealth has nothing to do with the color of your skin, the environment you came from, or whether you're a boy or a girl. It doesn't even have anything to do with how much money you're making.

It has everything to do with what you choose to do with the money you have, when you make it.

It's all in this book. And it will take only one moment for you to realize that everything you want is possible. When that moment happens, it is the most freeing feeling you will ever feel, because you will know that you have control over your life.

Take that control. And remember what Yoda said:

"Try not.
Do or do not.
There is no try."

ABOUT THE AUTHORS

Than Merrill

Than Merrill is one of the foremost real estate investors and educators in the country. The founder of CT Homes, LLC and FortuneBuilders, he is a nationally recognized expert in real estate investing, entrepreneurship, and marketing. A nationally sought-after speaker, Merrill has shared the stage with speakers such as former First Lady Laura Bush, Tony Robbins, Sarah Palin, and Robert Kiyosaki.

Born in Fresno, CA, Merrill attended Yale University, where he also played football. After graduating, he was drafted into the NFL and played with the Chicago Bears and Tampa Bay Buccaneers.

After his football career, Merrill transitioned his passion for football to real estate investing. Accordingly, he founded CT Homes, LLC, a real estate investment company, and FortuneBuilders, a real estate education company dedicated to giving students the training, resources, and systems to successfully invest in real estate. Merrill has authored two best-selling books on Amazon, *The Wholesaling Bible* and *The E-Myth Real Estate Investor*, and has also starred in A&E's hit reality TV show *Flip This House*.

With a strong passion for philanthropy, Merrill and his wife, Cindy, started the Equal Footing Foundation in 2010 with the mission of educating and promoting health and sports for youth. In 2013, Merrill and his company launched FortuneBuilders Gives in an effort to provide charitable and volunteering opportunities to employees, students, and local communities. Together with JP Servideo, Merrill launched Future FortuneBuilders in 2015 to help educate teens on financial literacy and entrepreneurship.

Merrill currently works as CEO of FortuneBuilders in sunny San Diego, California. He loves spending time with his family, which includes his wife, Cindy, and their children, Tyce and Sky. Outside of the office, Merrill spends most of his free time changing diapers, trying to figure out the cure for hair loss, and fighting to kick his coffee habit.

John "JP" Servideo

John "JP" Servideo is an entrepreneur, real estate investor, and award-winning youth speaker on a mission to empower teens personally and financially.

After barely graduating high school, Servideo—armed with an unparalleled work ethic—quickly climbed the corporate ladder and gained almost ten years of high-level management experience by the age of thirty. He also learned how the economy can affect your life after being laid off twice in that time and losing everything he'd worked so hard to gain.

Drawing on his natural East Coast resiliency and old-school Italian upbringing, Servideo picked himself back up, working with Olympic-athlete and multimillionaire mentors to learn how to achieve the highest levels of success in life.

Servideo dedicates his life to teaching others what he's learned, significantly influencing a generation for the better, helping the homeless, building multiple businesses, and living the life of his dreams—all while staying fit and seeking out new experiences in San Diego, California, and around the world.

Take Control with FortuneBuilders

Do you want to take control of your financial future?

Investing expert Than Merrill, founder of FortuneBuilders, has everything you need to achieve financial freedom through real estate. You have the opportunity to learn:

- The top real estate investing strategies for new or experienced investors
- How to invest on a part-time basis and take control of your time
- The power of systems and how to think like an entrepreneur
- How to utilize your retirement accounts to purchase real estate at a discount
- How to acquire the best income-producing properties that can generate cash flow every month
- And much more!

Than Merrill and FortuneBuilders offer live workshop events, online education, and one-on-one coaching to educate individuals on how to use real estate investing as the vehicle to help achieve ultimate financial freedom.

To learn more about FortuneBuilders events and

education, visit www.fortunebuilders.com or call (800) 815-5181.

You can also stay connected with Than Merrill by subscribing to his blog, www.ThanMerrill.com, and following him on social media:

Twitter: @thanmerrill
Instagram: @thanmerrill
Facebook: facebook.com/thanmerrill

Future FortuneBuilders

Are you ready to jump-start your financial education?

If you are between the ages of thirteen and seventeen or know someone who would be interested in furthering his or her financial knowledge, Future FortuneBuilders (FFB) is here to help!

- The financial trend across the nation shows consumer debt is at an all-time high
- 84 percent of students aged eighteen to twenty-five said that they needed financial management in high school
- Of those students, 54 percent said they wished they had access to financial management courses

Future FortuneBuilders (FFB) was created to close the gap in financial education. FFB runs financial literacy day camps for teens with the mission of providing its students with the fundamentals of personal finances and the financial concepts that will serve them for the rest of their lives.

To learn more about Future FortuneBuilders, how to attend a camp, or how to donate, visit our website: www.futurefortunebuilders.com.

You can also stay connected with our FFB team by following along on social media:

Instagram: @ffbcamp
Twitter: @ffbcamp

Get JP to Speak at Your School

Want JP Servideo to speak to your school, group, or organization?

JP is a nationally recognized motivational speaker. Crash one of his talks on success and learn how to

- Beat the "life lottery" of where you came from to find success

- Build habits that give you wealth and freedom

- Reverse-engineer goals to create your dream life

- Fail like a winner
- Find the people who already know how to get what you want

JP gives presentations to teens about

- Financial literacy
- Making good decisions
- Drugs and alcohol
- Motivation, confidence, and taking action
- Leadership
- Entrepreneurship
- . . . and many other topics.

JP also offers motivational presentations to parents of teens and speaks at corporate conferences. Along with motivation, he teaches parents what to teach their kids about money.

To hire JP to speak, visit www.jpservideo.com.

You can also stay up to date with JP by following him on social media:

Twitter: @jpservideo
Instagram: @jpservideo
Facebook: www.facebook.com/jpservideo